Sex Lies & Alibis

Exposing the Game to Transform Relationships

L. Dwain Boswell

Trussville, AL

Printed in the United States of America.

Freewill Publishers also publishes its books in a variety of electronic formats. Some content that appears in print may not be available in electronic books. For general information on other products and service, please e-mail info@freewillpublishers.com.

Cover design and inside layout: Guru Graphics, Inc.
Illustrator: Author
Editors: Eula Thompson and Angel Jones
ISBN 978-0-9848667-4-8
ISBN 978-0-9848667-5-5 (eBook)
Library of Congress Control Number: 2012936983

Public forum feedback for Sex Lies & Alibis

"I look at dating a whole new way now. I see time is needed for me to grow. I see what I want in someone else, but I need something to offer too." Female 18-20

"As I look back I realize I could have done things a whole lot differently. But that is the past. 'EXCELLENT!'" **Female 24-26**

"I've been friends with a guy for 8 years. We are best friends and talk at least 3 hours on the telephone everyday. We have decided to take things slow and not rush into the stages too soon. We have also made a commitment to not have sex until we are married." **Female 24-26**

"It has provided me with the information needed to help several people & friends. This is a God sent seminar" **Male 27-29**

"It has further helped me to seek out qualities within myself that need improvement or elimination. Also, I've also been able to examine how I handle situations with the opposite sex." **Female 24-26**

"This seminar reinforced a lot of topics that were already included in my personal studies, while still introducing a fresh perspective. There were a couple of times that I thought 'I never looked at it like that', and exploring another perspective from my own always encourages growth." **Female 24-26**

"I thought it to be extremely helpful because of a situation with a particular female I've been with. It was great!!" **Male 18-20**

"This seminar has helped me in my current relationship and my friends who I hang out with on a regular basis. My

boyfriend and I have talked and I have shared with him what I've learned and we are in agreement. Engagement is next!"Female 21-23

"It has helped me re-evaluate some of the relationships in my life." Female 18-20

"This seminar helped me to assess my current relationships and explained some issues I've had in the past." Female 21-23

"I really enjoyed this seminar. It has taught me a lot and will be a great tool to me." Female 18-20

CONTENTS

Part Two: Phasing Out the Game

ACKNOWLEDGMENTS

This book is sort of an anthropological study of over ten years that contrasts what I have termed as "the *culture* of the game" and what I am presenting as a new approach to successful relationships. The study began in the mid-nineties as I was failing in my own relationship. I am grateful for the wisdom gained, but I hope my bad experiences can be someone else's inspiration to do it right.

I am also grateful for the many students, friends, and colleagues who have attended the forums I have done on this topic and for the hundreds of youth, young adults, and parents who have given feedback and encouragement over the years to write this book.

I would like to especially acknowledge those to whom I feel a deep sense of love and gratitude:

— to my treasure of a wife and very best friend Renona, and to each of our wonderful children Adia and Matthew. You make it easy for me to teach principles that have been practiced in the home. Thanks for being the first to listen to my ideas and concepts and for supporting my desire to share this insight with others.

– to my parents Rev. Lewis and Elaine for your constant demonstrations of love that helped shape my honor for women and the marriage covenant. Even your imperfections made me a better man.

– to my sister Nyoka for your consistent love and motivation to go for it. You have always been a star in my eyes. I look forward to sharing the stage of life with you as we inspire in our own artistic ways.

INTRODUCTION

It is necessary to read the introduction since this book is so against the grain in its approach. I felt it was particularly beneficial to establish a foundation that would serve as the basis for this book. The first several chapters expose what I have observed over the past ten years as I watched and listened to people in relationships. Many of us have been engaged in a hit-or-miss dating process. I have learned that each generation has its own set of childhood and family experiences that contribute to its view of relationships. My childhood, for instance, from about age twelve was influenced by Crockett and Tubbs on Miami vice, The Cosby Show, Run-D.M.C., and Michael Jackson. As I grew into my teenage years, I was just starting to hear a whisper of the AIDS epidemic among my generation. And I overheard my parents talking about the Jimmy Bakker scandal and Jimmy Swaggart's sexual relations with prostitutes.

At the age of nineteen, I met my college sweetheart. The year was nineteen ninety two when Amy Fisher pleaded guilty to shooting her lover's wife, Mary Jo Buttafuoco. Joey Buttafuoco was convicted on statutory rape charges. Mike Tyson was found guilty of raping an eighteen year old Miss Black America contestant.[1] My sheltered "Cosby Show" perspective of a model family was bombarded with a dose of reality as my college peers debated what they considered being "she wanted it" vs. statutory rape.

This was a snippet of the *culture* from my generational perspective that influenced my view of relationships. My Cosby Show perspective continued to deteriorate morally and sexually as divorce rates climbed to over fifty percent. By age twenty, I had been totally overtaken by a dating culture with views that would continue to be reinforced by mass media.

Today, media influence is no longer restricted to newspapers, magazines, books, television or radio. Mass media have expanded to include blogs, message boards, podcasts, live text and video sharing that has taken media influence to another level. Everyone has the opportunity to blog their thoughts, post a facebook message or send an online "tweet." These new forms of media can take the old school debates between individuals to a potentially global audience. This expansion of mass media has connected the world to individual critical thinkers who now have a far reaching channel with which to influence the self-image of society. The day of the Cosby Show's model family has been gradually overlaid with pictures of the modern family, and this picture will influence the next generation's view of relationships much differently.

By the time I reached twenty-one, my parental history, past relationship experience and other social influences were just a few of many ingredients that went into what guided my thoughts and actions. Because of this mix, I knew I wanted to marry the most inexperienced virgin I could find. Every girl in between who did not fit that description was simply a temporary compromise that I regretfully used to secure an image that was deeply rooted in the migrating swarms of sociocultural influences and mass media representation.

Part one of this book is written to prepare you for a new approach to successful relationships. Ultimately, it expresses how we are all vulnerable to a distinct mix of outside forces that can sabotage the success of any relationship and how we must change the way we think in order to see the "culture of the game" for what it is worth; absolutely nothing.

Part two of this book is more focused on a solution than part one by contrasting the traditional relationship methods with what I believe is a much better way. I will present you with a new approach that is guaranteed to be worth every unconventional step outlined. This book is written to provoke your thinking towards things that you may not have given much thought. I encourage you to discuss the lessons and ideas in this book with others. I am hopeful that you will identify with those who are still buried in the pain of a devastating relationship, as well as with those who currently have successful relationships and do not mind sharing that they did not get there without working through many of the issues discussed in this book. Also, you will find helpful definitions in the glossary section to ensure that we have the same understanding of the key words and phrases that are italicized throughout this book. It is up to you to open your heart and mind to receive this truth that will change, encourage and inspire for generations to come.

Part One

THE CULTURE OF THE GAME

Chapter 1

EXPOSING THE GAME

Game On

If you did not read the introduction go back and start there. It will help you understand the basis for the rest of this book. For decades, guys in particular have affectionately referred to themselves as *pimps*, *players*, *macks*, *big ballers* and *shot callers*. This is terminology that helps to personify what I am calling "*the culture of the game*." When we play relationship games, it gives life to this culture. I've seen people play relationship games while the other person in the relationship had no idea that games were being played. Many can attest to the fact that when it comes to the culture of the game, you may not want to play it, but it wants to play you. In every way that you are exposed to the outside forces of this culture, the game is turned on, but do not worry. There is a way that you can turn it off.

Our exposures to this culture can socialize us to erroneous ways of thinking and behaviors that have become the norm in society. For instance, over the years I've talked to men who bragged about controlling women with fear. They called it "putting her in her place." Violence is one of many fear tactics that has become a cultural norm in relationships. However, I recommend a new normal which is to free a woman with love. It sounds like an easy concept, but the average woman does not trust a man who says "I love you" too early, so love itself can feel like a game. Culturally, a man hears those words to mean that a woman wants to have sex with him. What a "catch twenty-two" it can be for those looking for true love when the exact word itself has been culturally watered down. Do not be dismayed. True love has power, but mixing love with the culture of the game is like mixing oil with water. True love will always rise purely and unselfishly toward the surface where its actions can be seen, providing fuel for a relationship.

The culture of this world confuses love with two other L-words, "LUST" and what I call the "infamous LIST," which has become common as water. True love can conquer the game if it is allowed to be shown, much more, than if it is restricted to being said. When lust is involved, its intense sexual desire causes people to play games on purpose, but when the infamous list is involved, any intolerable violations of the list can turn a serious relationship into a dangerous game. Often, there is nothing anyone can do about violating something on someone's infamous list, and consequently, the average person doesn't know when he or she is in violation. Simply put, a potential mate is either checked-on or checked-off based on the list, possibly before a relationship gets started. Even when people know upfront that a relationship will eventually come to an end, their selfish attempt to fulfill their personal objectives can keep the game going, which usually leads to the typical violence and abuse before the relationship is finally severed.

The statistics on violence is a reflection of the unsuccessful fear tactics that all too often escalate into something deadly. According to the US Department of Justice, more than three women a day are murdered by their husbands or boyfriends in the United States. That equates to over one thousand women per year. Women experience two million injuries per year because of violence from what is supposed to be an intimate partner relationship. The way

I see it, one injured woman per year is too many. Further statistics suggest that those who were exposed to violence during their formative childhood years were more likely to become victims of dating violence. Many of us saw violence growing up either in our homes, at a family member's house, on TV, or within our own circle of friends as we aged out of our parent's house. This exposure continued to add to the mix of outside forces that shaped our thinking about relationships, whether we wanted it to or not.

Statistics are real, but a better reality is that you can beat the odds. You do not have to become a part of these statistics. I will continue to cite statistical evidence throughout this book, but only to support why the culture of the game is your enemy. My words at times may sound like I'm taking an episode out of your life, but do not take it personally, this is just a reflection of what I've observed in many relationships, including my own. And if the shoe fits, don't wear it because you will find out that when playing relationship games there are no winners. Someone may lose less, but no one ever wins.

What is The Game?

It should be obvious by now that I am not talking about monopoly, because somebody wins when playing that game. I'm not talking about video games like Madden football. I am not talking about tennis, golf, ping pong, pool, or tick tack toe. For the remainder of this book, we will refer to this game that has no winners as "The culture of the game" or simply, "the game." *Culture* is the total ways of living built up by a group of human beings and transmitted from one generation to another. It is the behavior and beliefs characteristic of a particular social, ethnic, or age group. Culture in and of itself is not observably wrong, but the culture of the game is characterized by negative patterns of behavior, symbolic attitudes, unbridled lust, pornography, explicit language, provocative clothing, seduction, drugs, intoxication, wild parties, immorality, envy, conflict, rivalry, jealousy, selfishness, character assassination, uninhibited sex, cheating, adultery, and the worship of money.[2] It is a collection of some of the worst sets of activities characteristic of human society around the world, which can be transmitted from one person to another like a sexual disease. It is a reflection of our worst imperfections, and we either behold ourselves in that reflection or smash the mirror in utter rejection. The culture of the game maintains such an "anything goes" mentality that it challenges not only our moral beliefs, but also the current and future laws of the land.

We are all vulnerable to our social environments in some way, and it is our instinct to survive and thrive in them. As a child, I lived in several different neighborhoods, and each one favored a certain walk and a certain talk. In order to survive socially, I had to adjust to those different environments. As an adult, my environment continues to change, but now I have developed some pretty decent survival skills that are more grounded by a strong set of core values. With each generation, there will always be new social influences that will change how individuals walk and talk. Surviving in our social environments now require a more advanced set of skills. Of course, you realize that the culture of the game is not necessarily packaged in a box and sold over the counter, but its span of influence is much more widespread. Instead, it is a bloodsucking parasite being hosted by TV, movies, music, magazines, internet and ultimately our society in general. Consequently, no matter where you live or where you are from, the game is an untouchable phenomenon that can be observed by anyone, anywhere in the world.

When it comes to the game, just surviving is not enough; we need immunity in order to become fortified against this parasitic culture. Usually, when an immune system is exposed to an agent that is foreign to the body, it will develop the ability to fight off any future attacks, but that is not what has happened with regard to the game. Relationships are being plagued by a cultural virus, and many of us have acquired an immune deficiency of the soul. Many minds have been conformed to this culture; others may have lost the will to resist the culture and some are so emotionally drained that they have no hope. This book has the potential to restore your hope by providing a sense of immunity from the culture of the game and a way to succeed in your relationships. The following are a few definitions of key terms and phrases that will help us move forward together with the same understanding as we work towards this immunity.

- **The game:** an active interest or pursuit that focuses on personal fulfillment as the object of victory.
- **The objective:** anything relative to personal fulfillment, whether it is amusement, entertainment, pleasure, financial, or simply to pass the time.
- **To play games:** to act in a deceitful, lying, manipulative, or evasive manner.
- **The culture of the game:** a competitive or challenging pursuit involving skill, chance, and endurance on the part of two or more persons who play according to no set of rules, usually for their own personal fulfillment or for the perceived approval of other spectators.

I want to reiterate some key points from that last bullet which should help you understand why the game has no winners. Even if you set out to win, how can you win if you do not know who else is playing? Someone in the relationship will always be in the dark especially when that third, fourth or fifteenth person enters the game. People who play games do not want you to know about others with whom they are playing the field. If you are the player or the victim, either way you will lose. If you are just in a relationship for personal fulfillment, the most you can say is that it was good while it lasted. The problem with that statement is that you have to give something to get something, and what you got is more than likely not worth what you gave up. Eventually the light bulb comes on revealing that the spectators' approval we so desperately wanted is not what we perceived it would be. Time, money, virtue, or anything else you feel is owed to you can not be redeemed, because no one plays the game by any set of rules. The following is a real example of how these elements can play out in a relationship.

Two college students meet for the first time. To protect their identity let's call them Fred and Wilma. Both are physically attracted to each other. They start out tremendously flirty and seductive to let the other know that they are interested. A short period of time goes by as their attraction for one another leads to frequent dinner dates at a restaurant near campus. Variations of verbal compliments are passed across the table, as a lustful trance envelops the room. It seems as if no one else is around but the two of them. They begin to interpret one another's nonverbal communication to gauge whether or not their personal fulfillment objectives can be met. Neither knows what the other is after, but both share intense feelings of physical attraction. He may be wondering how her juicy red lips taste. She may be taken away by how muscular his arms look and can't wait for him to wrap them around her. These strong desires begin to weaken their natural defense against the culture of the game. Fred pays for dinner as they start a progression that quickly moves from just kissing in the car; to cuddling on the couch; to sex in the bedroom; where Shakespeare's world famous eight limbed sex monster with two backs finally takes its form between the sheets.

Remember, the objective of the game is anything relative to personal fulfillment. Weeks go by, and one person may have met their objective. Maybe for the guy it was just sex. Maybe for the girl it was companionship. Who knows? It could be a need for a place to stay, room and board is expensive, maybe he is a means of transportation or material resources, maybe he has a large network and his popularity equals her popularity or maybe she is remarkably smart and he needs her help to make it through school. The bottom line is that personal fulfillment is never disclosed, and it is just a matter of time before someone, usually the female, tries to apply rules to a relationship that is being fueled by personal fulfillment, rather than love.

When rules are imposed on someone who is heavily influenced by the culture of the game, it causes the mental, emotional and physical violence we see in relationships. Questions get asked such as, "What are we doing?" and "What am I to you?" These are questions that every "player" in the game knows will lead to the dreadful discussion about becoming exclusive. Wait a minute! Wouldn't you already be exclusive? Isn't it implied when two people agree to move the relationship between the sheets? Absolutely not! Implication helps to fuel relationship games, but rules govern conduct, action, and arrangements. Why would anyone need exclusivity when his or her personal fulfillment objective is already being met? At some point in the relationship, someone will try to establish rules. I have noticed that it is the female who usually initiates the conversation, as we fast forward a few weeks into Fred and Wilma's relationship.

Wilma sees Fred with several other girls around

campus and starts to get suspiciously jealous. She approaches Fred and says, "I don't want you hanging out with that girl anymore. I don't like her." Fred responds with, "She's just a friend. You have friends, and I'm not telling you who to hang out with." Wilma wants to define her relationship with Fred, so she attempts to lay down some rules which escalate into an argument. In order to salvage the relationship, Fred reluctantly agrees not to talk to that one girl anymore. Overtime, they eventually agree to only see each other. Fred never intended to become exclusive, but he was not ready to give up the sexual objective he was getting fulfilled. As the months go by, the rules become more and more restrictive, and Wilma's jealousy and insecurity continues to surface. Arguments become more and more intense, which leads to violence and verbal abuse. Their personal fulfillment objectives are starting to become less important. Neither knows how to have a successful relationship and quite frankly, neither probably wanted to become so serious at this point in their young lives. The culture of the game had plenty of time to influence their idea of relationships long before they ever met, and the newly imposed rules have only served to make things worse.

When a relationship is influenced by the culture of the game and someone wants to establish rules, you will experience intense friction in that relationship, because where there are no rules there will be chaos. I've noticed both in high school and college that there is more of a code than rules. For example, some guys referred to single ladies as fair game because relationships were considered to be a spectator's sport. Although, they do not want the girls to know that they were playing games, they do want the other guys to know that they do have game. Sex was obviously one of the most common personal fulfillment objectives, and still is. It was like a notch on a guy's sexual belt, an invisible panty belt that every so called "player" wore. In my experience, I am able to talk to other guys under this stereotypical unspoken male code where perception is more important than reality. As a matter of fact, I do not have to say a word. The typical guy is on a mission to earn man points with me without first finding out if I even care. Over the years, I noticed that guys perceived that the largest number of man points was received anywhere in the neighborhood of sexual exaggeration. No matter where I've looked or listened, guys who purposefully played relationship games saw women as nothing more than sexual trophies, some of which were in different leagues.

Players and Victims

Contrary to popular belief, all men are not dogs and all women are not gold diggers. There are two sides to this so called "game," victims of the game and players of the game. Victims do not intend to play games, but may get caught in it like a fly in a web. Victims are deceived and cheated by the dishonesty of others. I am convinced that victims do not want to play relationship games, but relationships have a way of revealing deep internal issues from the unfortunate mix of our past, that we did not know about ourselves. For example, in our cultural mix it is not cool to be a virgin. Therefore, some people are persuaded by the idea that sex sells and will use sex as a trade off for something else they may want.

Sometimes the culture of the game becomes a way of saving face, like wearing a mask, or pretending to like, want, and do things to avoid embarrassment. Ultimately, this embarrassment perpetuates that culture, a culture that gives people something to hide their internal issues behind. Being heavily influenced by the culture of the game is like being given the wrong driving directions, but it is your relationship that is taking the wrong turn.

"Players," however, embrace relationship games and are actively looking for their next victim. Players often have a calculated strategy, approach, or scheme. Their thoughts are predetermined and premeditated. Players play games on purpose. For those who relate to being a player keep reading, and this book just might open your eyes. For those of you who relate to being a victim, this book will become your guide. Many of you have sighed deeply, longing for a better way to do relationships; a way that allows more control over the craziness in today's dating culture; a way that provides some defense against the games that people play. Maybe you feel there is just no way around relationship games. Keep reading and you will find that there is a better way.

Where is The Game Played?

Some games such as monopoly are played on boards. Other games are played on fields, screens, tables, water, etc. Again, these are all games I would win. However, the game I'm talking about has no winners. People all over the world know what it means to "play the field." That phrase probably has international renown, which in my opinion, makes it a multicultural phenomenon. Where is this proverbial field? You probably already know that the playing field is the mind. Many people have commonly referenced it in books, articles, songs, etc. I agree with the fact that playing games start in the mind. I am not endeavoring to get into psychoanalysis, however, with the next few paragraphs of this book I simply want to show the connection to the culture of the game and how easily it can affect your thinking if you are not firmly set against it.

The mind is a powerful element that enables us to be aware of the world and our experiences and to think and to feel. The mind is so powerful, it can function to influence your actions consciously and unconsciously (some prefer the word subconsciously, both meaning without your awareness). The mind also has a conscience that stores and maintains a moral sense of right and wrong. No matter what state of mind we are in, our actions can be influenced in either mental state. In consideration of the fact that man is a spirit and has a soul and both the spirit and soul resides in a physical body, the thoughts that produce actions can be influenced by any of these three parts of our existence.[3] Let's take a closer look at each of these components.

One can be influenced by the soul, which includes the conscious mind, the unconscious mind, the conscience, the will, and the emotions. When my actions are influenced by my will, they are deliberate actions of choice requiring mental effort, which is consciously controllable. According to Bargh & Chartrand, the conscious process has remained consistent and stable for over 100 years.[4] Some may refer to people as having a strong or weak will, but either way, that action has to be a conscious decision in order to be regarded an act of the will. For instance, if a wife finds out that her husband has cheated with another woman, and the husband says he did not mean it, the implication is that his actions were influenced by something other than a conscious state of mind because the will to do something can only exist in consciousness.

Apart from some disorder, in order for a husband to end up sexually involved with another woman, one would have to conclude that he deliberately chose the path of action that led to his infidelity. In other words, it was a conscious act of the will; therefore, he meant to do it.

The important question then becomes "what is he going to do about the desire?" If we rewind to the point in time where that same husband was asked, "Do you take this woman to be your lawfully wedded wife?" the response "I will" was not an unconscious response. The words "I will" represented a conscious vow to have and to hold only one woman with an emotional and sexual bond. This conscious intention of a person exercising his or her will in favor of another is far more gratifying than being forced or required. Simply put, no married couple was unconscious when they vowed before God, "I Will." Understand that spiritually, God gave us the free will to choose Him. If people were forced or required to choose God, there would be no *sovereignty* in God, and our loyalty to God would be questionable.

The body, however, can be influenced by the entirety of the soul as described above. Moreover, the body can also be influenced by the spirit, as well as the faculties of the body such as touch, sight, smell, hearing, or taste. These senses combined can be used to perceive something originating either within or outside the body. The unconscious mind interacts with conscious reasoning, allowing the body and soul the capacity to respond to whatever signals it receives. Therefore, we all have habits, reactions, and dreams that seem to operate independently of our will. For instance, have you ever put shaving cream in the hand of a person who is sleeping and tickled their nose with a feather? It is so hilarious when they slap themselves in the face with shaving cream and wake up to what feels like a surreal moment.

I know because it has happened to me. I reacted to what I felt, even though it was not a conscious act of my will to slap myself in the face with shaving cream. This is what I call a low level of thinking, unconscious thoughts that produce somewhat involuntary reactions. Many people live their lives in this manner, constantly being controlled by thoughts that have been given free reign in both their subconscious and conscious minds for so long that there is little to no resistance built up against those thoughts. Their actions simply become programmatic, like an old tape playing in the background of their mind saying respond this way.

I believe we were all born with a blank tape that represented a morally good conscience, but along the way it can get seared by extreme exposure to this low level of thinking that is evident in the culture of the game.[5] When we are not selective to what we allow our eyes to see and ears to hear, what was once immoral can start to seem morally OK; our morally good tapes become re-written with recordings of things we once rejected. We become mentally desensitized, which gradually lowers our mindset to a cold and hard unconscious or subconscious level of acceptance. As this desensitizing continues, our thoughts are lowered where right and wrong are no longer even considered, and we lose our conscious will to define what we will and will not allow in our own little worlds. Again, this is why you need to be firmly set against the culture of the game. It is a powerfully desensitizing force.

Since actions can be influenced by a very low level of thinking, then the opposite must also be just as true. Over time, actions can be influenced by a high level of thinking.

Let's turn now to a very high level, which is what I am touting to be your defense, your immunity, and your way around the culture of the game. You are a spirit, you have a soul and both reside in a physical body. This makes up the whole you, but in order to have immunity from the game, your spirit has to be the primary influencer of your thoughts because essentially, you are a spirit. We are not a mind or a body, but a human spirit. Our spirit is what sets us apart from dogs, cats, monkeys and other animals. Each of our human spirits is either influenced by the high and powerful Spirit of God or the low and evil spirit of Satan, who I refer to as the enemy of our mind, will and emotions. Your body will betray you and your mind has its limitations, but when discerning good and evil, the human spirit is the only part of you that can consistently receive discernment between the two, because it is the only part of you that can connect with the Spirit of God.[6]

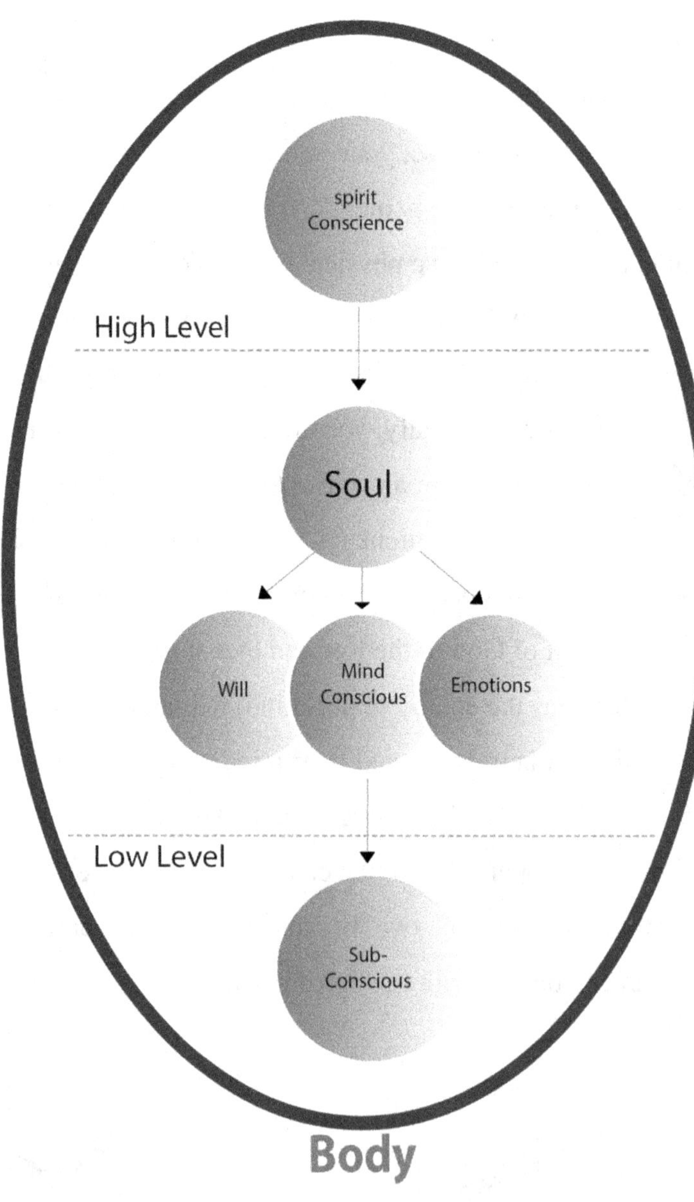
spirit
Conscience
High Level
Soul
Will
Mind
Conscious
Emotions
Low Level
Sub-
Conscious
Body

Bite Size

- When it comes to the culture of the game, you may not want to play it, but it wants to play you. Game on!
- Relationships are being plagued by a cultural virus, and many of us have acquired an immune deficiency of the soul.
- The culture of the game maintains such an "anything goes" mentality, that it challenges not only our moral beliefs, but also the current and future laws of the land.
- When rules are imposed on someone who is heavily influenced by the culture of the game, it causes the mental, emotional and physical violence we see in relationships.
- Where there are no rules there will be chaos.
- When lust is involved, people will play games on purpose, but when the infamous list is involved, any intolerable violations of the list can turn a serious relationship, into a dangerous game.
- True love will always rise purely and unselfishly toward the surface where its actions can be seen, providing fuel for a relationship.

Chapter 2

A 3D VIEW

The Illusion

Since we have covered a good portion of what I've described as the culture of the game, you should be ready for my 3D view of the game. The term 3D is typically a reference to a motion picture that enhances the illusion of depth perception. 3D films are said to be relatively costly and lack the standardized format for all segments of the entertainment industry. Lately, I've seen 3D technology used in some of the most awkward films. It is as if filmmakers are brandishing 3D technology to get an edge in the competitive motion-picture industry, and movie goers have started to expect it. The culture of the game reminds me of various elements of a 3D film.

First, as with a 3D film, the culture of the game is a projection of an illusion. The self-image of society is always changing based on the influence of mass media hype. Millions of people are subject to its misleading sounds and images that have impaired our view of reality. For example, the high profile polygamist method of dating has added depth to the illusion that marriage is a temporary arrangement. So temporary that divorce has become a hugely profitable business in the United States.

Second, expensive advertisement and promotions are often laced with subliminal messages which perpetuate the culture of the game. These messages contribute to unrealistic relationship expectations which are rooted in sexual fantasies. I want to make the case that fantasy will never be reality, but it is almost a moot point since many people do not want to accept reality. Regardless, I will give it my best shot.

Failed relationships increase the potential of contracting sexually transmitted diseases as people move from one person to the next. These failed relationships are the precursor to failed marriages, which continue to fuel the increasing divorce rates. The reality is that marriage and relationships take work that many people are not willing to put in, and the culture of the game can blind us from that reality. According to maritalstatus.com, a website geared toward divorce and remarriage, divorce is a twenty-eight billion dollar a year industry, with an average cost of about twenty thousand dollars. A decline in the divorce rate would negatively impact that industry's profit. Why would such industries and the powers that be want to see relationships succeed when failed relationships are a much more profitable paradox?

Thirdly, as with 3D films, the culture of the game is not the standard format for all segments of society. I am advocating that playing games should not be the standard for any segment. However, many dating couples have embraced the game, expecting it to play out in some form or fashion, at least until they are ready to "settle down." Then of course, all players in the game must somehow cut off any extra relationships, along with any mental and emotional ties. This is an unrealistic standard in a society that has been set by what is common, normal or profitable. Many industries are established around this standard, one that hurts people for profit. For example, ABCNews.com reported that pornography has grown into a ten billion dollar business, and the performers are hired as young as eighteen to have sex that is often unprotected. This industry quietly feeds profits to cable and satellite companies, production companies, hotels, and the internet- you name it. The pornography business is bigger than the NFL, NBA and Major League Baseball combined.[7] Why wouldn't the profiteers want to make this more of a normal part of society?

I regard the pornography industry to be a laboratory that is purposefully becoming more explicit in order to make social attitudes more tolerant. When people become more tolerant it makes it easier to push the definition of obscenity in law further out, which allows for even more extremism in the industry. It also breeds an insatiable sexual appetite and inspires the hideous thoughts that manifest itself in such actions as rape, prostitution and human sex trafficking. This is especially true with regard to the exploitation of young women and children that are forcefully being served to sick men like lab rats. This is what viewing the uncommon as common has done to our society. We must refuse to allow the dating culture to become the standard for how we do relationships. What's normal can no longer be set by the general standards of society. If you start today by establishing and following a set of guiding principles that protect rather than hurt people, your perception of what is normal will never be compromised by profit.

Of course, I am using the term 3D as a play on words. It is a reference to the illusion that the culture of the game projects which can influence how we act in relationships. Going forward, I want you to remember three words that actually begin with the letter "D": denounce, discern, and dodge. These three words will help express various points of view about how to avoid the game altogether.

We've heard that a threefold cord is not quickly broken. In other words, the strength of all three cords bound together is greater than any one of the cords used separately. This is known as synergy. An outstanding example of synergy is the fact that one horse can pull six tons, while two horses can pull thirty-six tons. If we did not see this happen, we would almost think it was indeed an illusion. Mathematically, one would predict that two horses would be limited to pulling double what one horse could pull, which is twelve tons, but the interaction of the two horses has an effect that is six times more powerful than that of any single horse pulling on its own. As I continue towards my goal of convincing you that the culture of the game should be avoided all together, I ask that you will help me spread this 3D view so as to harness the power of synergy.

The First D

Professional teachers are trained to use a system of rules called mnemonics [ni-mon-iks], which includes several things such as formulas and rhymes as a technique to assist the memory. It is not only effective, but a fun way to help people remember key points. My understanding of this technique is why I chose to use three words that start with the letter “D.” Going forward, I hope you will always see the game from this “3D” perspective. The first “D” in the 3D view is to totally and openly DENOUNCE the game, meaning to give it up, disapprove of it, and to condemn it. Denounce is a strong word that drives home the essence of what I want you to do with this culture. Denounce means to get out of something altogether. Namely, getting out of the game, which requires awareness that this culture exists, because you can’t denounce what does not exist. Denouncing the game is like identifying an enemy of war, you should always be on the lookout for your enemy. I have said emphatically that the culture of the game is your enemy. If you do not agree with that statement, hopefully you will by the end of this book.

Denouncing the game requires courage to deal with tough issues beginning in the early phase of a relationship. This will allow you to cut your losses early and quickly move on to the man or woman that is right for you. It is a waste of your time to uncover lies in the later phase of a relationship, especially if it has led to marriage, because you will then have to live with those lies for an undetermined amount of time before becoming a part of the unfortunate divorce statistics. Yes, you can beat the odds, but your chances are much greater if you denounce the game.

My daughter was ten years of age at the time I started writing this book. Being the father of an innocent, precious little girl has changed the way I view the world. Especially, since I would give my life to protect my daughter. This whole idea of denouncing the game is a reflection of the ongoing conversation I have regularly with both my kids. One question that challenged me to test the concepts in this book came from my daughter during one of our weekly talks. She asked, "Daddy, when will I be able to date… I mean, what age?" Wow, what a question to ask the most loving and protective dad in the world! I stopped and thought silently, not expecting her to ask that question so soon. It may sound like an easy question to answer given the current trends, but it wasn't. It crossed my mind to say sixteen, maybe seventeen, but it just wouldn't come out. This is my precious daughter asking this question. My daughter hangs on every word I say. If I had said never, she would have asked why, while reverently taking me serious. I had to get this answer right.

What I knew about dating began to replay in my mind during that moment of silence. I thought about the girls my friends and I dated in our day. I thought how progressively worse the culture of the game has become. I thought about the fact that ninety-five percent of Americans experience sex before marriage! I thought about how the average age people experience premarital sex has dropped from age twenty to age seventeen for those born between 1982 and 1997 (often referred to as generation Y). I worried that if the trend continued, my ten-year-old daughter and eight-year-old son's generations would start experiencing premarital sex on average at age fifteen! All within a moment, one question fast forwarded my thinking five years into the future. Although I wanted to respond with a resounding NEVER, I looked into the sweet face of the most beautiful little girl I have ever seen and took a deep breath.

So what did I tell her? I simply answered her question with the following question: "What's the point in dating someone that you wouldn't want to marry?" My daughter answered, "There isn't one." I was so proud to hear that answer. She got it! She realized that dating, talking, going steady, courting - whatever your generation calls an exclusive boyfriend and girlfriend relationship - is not something you do for the fun of the game. I immediately followed up with the idea of seeing people as friends instead of someone to couple off with just for the fun of it. I reinforced her answer with the freedom to go on dates, yes dates with an "s," whenever she got ready, as long as the guy was a friend and not an exclusive boyfriend soiling her goods until he finds his true love. Since that conversation, a thirteen year old student at her school became pregnant, and we were able to discuss consequences in light of a real life situation. I can't control whether or not she follows my advice, but I can expose the danger of picking up all the unhealthy emotions, which are inevitably found in the sexually promiscuous culture of the game.

In order to equip her with a new way of thinking about relationships, I explained that she should spend time with friends who do not want to receive anything in return but her friendship. We continued to discuss the dating question from that perspective as I shared with her my approach to a successful relationship. I will go into further details of this approach in the second half of this book, but for now, I just want you to denounce the game. My daughter may not have verbalized it in the way I will in this book, but she is on the right track. My goal is to convince her that the future success of her relationships requires that she stays out of enemy territory by totally denouncing the culture of the game.

The Second D

There are many signals in relationships that will let you know if someone is playing games. Often, we do not see these red flags because our view is limited by emotional and sexual blinders or simply the idea of falling in love. Taking any blinders off that limit your ability to see the person behind the mask will help you expand your peripheral vision so you can better DISCERN the game.

The second D is learning to DISCERN the game which means to recognize. The most practical way to recognize the game is to pay close attention to the character of a person. Character gives you a glimpse into what has become a part of a person's nature whether they are courageous, adventurous, affectionate, faithful, or anything in between. Honesty and integrity, for instance, are character traits we can observe, but in order for such traits to become the individual nature of a person, one must continuously live honestly and walk in integrity. This observation is just as practical as recognizing that a building has been condemned. If you see a building with yellow "caution" tape restricting its entrance, you should quickly recognize that the building is unsafe. As you further evaluate the characteristics of the building, you may notice that its windows and doors are boarded up. When a building is condemned it naturally becomes the breeding ground for other problems. In the same way that a condemned building has recognizable characteristics that give insight into its safety, so do people. The problem is that we can't distinguish when we are getting into an unsafe relationship because unsafe people are not walking around with caution signs draped across their chests. Nevertheless, when we focus on a person's character, like an optical illusion, a caution sign will eventually come into focus. It is your responsibility not to pull the relationship trigger too quickly, but to allow yourself enough time to focus in on a person's true nature. This book will help re-train you to focus on the character of people, so that your eyes will be opened to see the potential danger lurking behind a cute face.

Discern also means to distinguish which takes the word recognition a step further. Let's imagine that you are facing the most attractive, state-of-the-art building that is standing just next to a condemned building. If you had to go potty right now, which one of these buildings would you rather enter? You may be thinking, what kind of question is that? Well, indulge me for just a moment. Would you go up to the condemned building and rip away the "caution" tape? Would you pull the "keep out" sign off the door in order to gain access? Would you somehow pry a board off the window and climb through, so that you could use the bath room inside the condemned building? I can hear you saying, absolutely not! No one in his or her right mind would do such a thing. Unless your mental state has been altered by some type of drug, or psychological problem, most people can see how unattractive and dangerous the above scenario would be.

A condemned building with no running water or other working utilities has many hazards that would threaten your safety. I'm sure you can see the danger and risk associated with hazardous material, but many people have a problem seeing the culture of the game as hazardous, mainly because the game is covered with what has become a very attractive facade. Its projections look and sound so pretty that some people fail to recognize what's going on behind the scenes. The game is like starring at a condemned building that has been covered over with new external walls and a new facing, but underneath the facade it is reeking with rotten, decaying, hazardous material; such hazards as HIV/AIDS, abusive behavior, low self-esteem, or extreme insecurity. Over time, these and other hazardous elements will eat away at the internal support until nothing is left but an empty, hollow, fragile shell of a person.

I challenge you right now to tune your radio to almost any station, and count the number of songs that talk about what he will do, she is doing, or they could do sexually. Sex is not something you do in a talent show. Sex is not something you put on your resume. Yet, in the culture of the game, how a person performs in bed is talked about as if it is the glue of the relationship. These types of references to sex add to the external facade of freshly painted walls and decorative storefront facings that cover how damaged this old reused relationship culture is. Engaging in sex simply as a physical and seductive act has become the most important animating principle of this world. It is as if sex is the center of thought, feeling, and motivation, both consciously and unconsciously directing the body's reactions through its social and physical existence. Since sex is so much more than a physical act, I have devoted an entire chapter to the reality that great sex is more internal than external. For now, I'm only talking about how sex is used in the culture of the game.

In our culture, we all know sex sells. It is like the complimentary basket of bread that finds its way to your restaurant table just before you place your order. The waiter sees you as a statistic that says the average person that eats at this restaurant will want a basket of bread; therefore, there is no need to make any distinction between the average customer and the few who do not want bread right? Of course not, this is how the thought of what's normal or acceptable gets forced on aggregates of the population as if there is no other option. Almost like a basket of bread, the culture of the game will come your way, whether you want it to or not. The upside is that you have the power to distinguish yourself, to denounce it, to push away that basket of sexually glamorized, puffy fantasies and embrace the reality of what a healthy and successful relationship requires.

Among the people who are in a relationship, or actively seeking a relationship, I have not seen much consideration in favor of or against a person on the basis of what he or she believes. This is one of the most fundamental realities of a healthy relationship, but as long as the physical and sexual attraction is there, the average couple simply do not concern themselves with core values, character and convictions. If sex happens to lead to a child together, their different views on religion alone tend to cause conflict over issues such as how to raise that child. It amazes me how critical this issue becomes to raise kids with values that were not displayed in their hyper-sexual relationship. When couples get into relationships based purely on physical and sexual attraction, initially there is little conversation about beliefs and values. They are usually blind to the convictions of the other, and any subsequent love child often leads to a battle over what values will be instilled into that child. Simply put, their fake fantasies are now being forced to surrender to a very real reality.

It should be quite obvious that women are somewhat targeted for sex. Men are targeted also, but very few women target men for the purpose of sex. The female players typically target men for money, status, fame, security or other material reasons. Very few men target women for anything other than sex. Either way, both men and women are targeted for whatever the personal fulfillment objective is, making the need to discern the game even more important. Understand that discernment works both ways, some people recognize the game in order to play it, and others recognize the game in order to avoid it. Your goal should always be to avoid the game altogether, and the first step towards accomplishing that is to distinguish yourself from it.

Your character can distinguish and set you apart, or you can allow it to be tainted by the culture of the game. You do not have to embrace any societal norm that goes against who you are. There is enough duplication going around, and being different is as normal as you are going to get. As a matter of fact, your differences are the most distinctive things about you. Once you have a mindset to distinguish yourself, you will be more aware and attract others who are also distinguished. What can be better than when two people come together recognizing that the game is not their friend, who single themselves out and honor themselves? They would be two people who are prime candidates to expect the best in their relationship. Such course of action should bring them to the realization that denouncing the game and discerning the game are extremely rewarding.

The Third D

I understand that sex is a vitally important part of our state of being, but sex should not be our god. This is exactly what some people have made it. They are opening their spirit, soul and body to a culture that is consumed by sexual fantasies, obscene writings, racy photographs, and exotic films that have little or no artistic merit. Erotic inclinations have not only become more obvious in the music culture, but also in mainstream commercials. No matter where you look or listen, whether primetime TV or radio, something erotic will bombard your eyes and ears, gradually depleting the little virtue that is left in our society if no one stands up against it. The pattern is evident, once the initial shock wears off more sex appeal and profanity are introduced until it becomes what is considered "socially acceptable." Primetime networks seem to have craftily desensitized the industry to instances of foul offensive language such as "son of a b!%@#, vulgar language such as "a**" or "a**hole", sexually suggestive language and censored language so partially bleeped out that it may as well have been spoken, “Fu** (bleep!).” Again, my children have drastically changed my view of the world.

Would you be ok if your elementary school kid came home from school and said, "I am so tired, I just want to sit my a** down. But I can't because my teacher gave me too much f***ing homework. She is such a b!%@#." I would be outraged as would many other parents, but this is exactly what kids can glean from mainstream media.

Why do nipple patches and strategic nipple-blurring make it acceptable to show naked breast on primetime TV? Or, if a nipple is "mistakenly" shown the only recourse to relatively inappropriate broadcasting is to publish an insincere apology or correction that does not undo the damage. How long before what's being apologized for becomes common place? "I'm sorry I said b!%@# on prime-time TV; oh, that is acceptable now, disregard my apology." All of this contributes to the language and behavior that is evident in the culture of the game, which is further magnified through relaxed mass media regulations.

Once you have denounced the game, you are better able to discern the game because you are keenly aware that it exists. The third D is ultimately to DODGE the game altogether because the culture of the game is inevitably going to come your way. I can't hide my daughter from this culture unless I lock her in the bedroom and slide food under her door for the rest of her life. Even if that was the case, what is left of moral humanity would eventually find me out and rescue her back into its immoral society, so that my daughter could get her fair share of the culture that everyone else is getting. Or, someone else's iPod will be filled with songs that have sexually explicit and violent lyrics. Apart from my supervision, someone will stick an ear plug in my son's ear and say, "listen to this." Therefore, the only recourse I have is to teach my kids this 3D view of the game, so that when mass media mania bombards their eyes and ears with lies, both will be able to stand against the culture.

Bite Size

- The self-image of society is always changing based on the influence of mass media hype. Millions of people are subject to its misleading sounds and images that have impaired our view of reality.
- We must refuse to allow the dating culture to become the standard for how we do relationships. What's normal can no longer be set by the general standards of society.
- The reality is that marriage and relationships take work that many people are not willing to put in, and the culture of the game blinds us from that reality.
- Denouncing the game requires courage to deal with tough issues beginning in the early phase of a relationship. This will allow you to cut your losses early and quickly move on to the man or woman that is right for you.
- Once you have DENOUNCED the game, you are better able to DISCERN the game because you are keenly aware that it exists. The third D is ultimately to DODGE the game altogether because the culture of the game is inevitably going to come your way.

Chapter 3

THE SOURCE OF THE GAME

An Evil Nature

Since the game is played in the mind, it is easy to conclude that the source of the game is lying. When a person meets someone whose nature turns out to be dangerously different from who he or she appeared to be, that false impression is a result of deception. When someone's spouse is unfaithful, you can find deception at the root of it. Have you ever been lied to? Have you ever caught someone in the middle of a lie? I'm sure you have. How did that make you feel? Were you angry? If you let it, can that anger carry over into a new relationship? Absolutely, I've seen it happen. When you understand that lying is the source of the game, you can then see why the game is inevitably going to come your way. Many of us can relate to the fact that we live in a world where people tell lies. Even I told lies at one point in my past, and I'm one of the good guys.

Let me give you a personal example of how I constantly have to denounce the game. My wife and I have a wonderful relationship, but there are times when I've had a challenging day, week, month and even year. Life is real; therefore, a relationship must be based on reality. I went home one day feeling as though life had me on the ropes, and I was losing the fight. My wife noticed my demeanor and asked, "What's wrong?" Although I looked and sounded like something was wrong, I inadequately responded, "nothing", as if I was powerless and she was the one draining me of my power. At that very moment when I said, "nothing," I failed to denounce the game. I failed to discern the game. Therefore, I failed to dodge the game. I was now playing games with my wife because, in fact, something was wrong. It was written all over my face, yet, I responded with a lie.

I went away prepared to have a pity party with myself, but shortly after, my wife crashed my party and pressingly inquired again, "What's wrong?" After going back and forth with the same lie about nothing being wrong, it finally hit me like a ton of bricks. I was playing games! Haven't we all done that at least once? So I had to check myself.

Even something as understanding as not wanting to burden my wife with the challenges of my day can send a mixed message that perpetuates the game. By arbitrarily telling a small lie, I was digging myself into a large pit. I could have told my wife the truth. I could have said, "Give me a minute to compose myself, and I will tell you what is going on." If I had done that, it would have been game over, and I could have avoided the game altogether.

I want you to see how lying can be taken for granted, and the more we lie the more we become desensitized to its evil nature. The more we become desensitized to lies, the more it will become a part of our nature, and once lying has become a part of our nature it will become a part of our character as a person. Your whole system of existence can become governed by tendencies to lie. Even if we want to be truthful, we find ourselves stuck in the realm of what should have been said, or could have been done.

In any relationship, characteristics such as honesty and integrity are vital. If you knew ahead of time that a person was a compulsive liar, I do not think you would enter into a close relationship with that person. With that said, I understand that people have a variety of things that constitutes truth. Seventy-two percent of people in American between ages 18 and 25 believe that there is no absolute truth, and truth is where many people come to a crossroads in their relationships.[58]

Truth is radically different from a lie and is the opposing force that must be used to combat lying. When I lied to my wife by saying "nothing," that response was completely opposite the true. A lie is very easy to dispute because one can not verify what did not happen or does not exist. Truth is easier to prove because one can verify reality. An American rapper by the name of Tupac Shakur said, "Only God can judge me" in one of his songs. It was an implication that he felt as though people were judging him. Of course that statement would resonate with most since people hold grudges; people have jealousy; people hate; and people have resentment towards others. To agree with Tupac's reference of the bible, I must say that only God has the power and capability to judge me as well. If I believed that people would be allowed to judge my eternal fate, I would be very afraid to face my judgment. Even those who believe that there is no absolute truth would probably opt to stand before God instead of their own neighbor, because neighbors not only tell lies, but are prone to believe lies that are told. To say that only God can judge me is a very sensible statement to make.

Unlike some, I believe the word of God is true from the beginning. It says to be sanctified through the truth.[8] Sanctify means to be set apart. Truth sets us apart from what opposes it, which is anything that is based on a lie. The bible refers to the Holy Spirit as the Spirit of truth who will guide you into all truth. It is therefore impossible to stay caught up in the culture of the game if you are being guided by the truth, because truth is a force that pushes away from its opposing force. Truth and lying have a sort of magnetic repulsion although they are as different as north and south. Opposites are supposed to attract, right? I like to think of it like this, lying is an attempt to pass off something as the truth, so people have to make their lie look and sound as similar to the truth as possible. Therefore, liars are repulsive, attempting to change their repulsive lies into attractive deception. Is there anything more repulsive and disgusting than being deceived into thinking you are dealing with the truth, when all along it was a lie? This is why the person who lies and the person who was deceived usually find themselves far removed from each other when all is said and done. I believe the truth will make you free, but only if you learn it, believe it and live it. One can not help but be free from anything that is based on a lie when truth is a value in their life. That includes being free from the game. However, I must reiterate, that you have to first get to the point where you value the truth. Once you start to value the truth, it will become a part of your good nature, and you will push away from anything that is based on a lie, a sort of spiritual magnetic repulsion.

Why People Lie

Most of us want to hear something comforting. No one wants to hear how fat he or she is while struggling to lose weight, or how sick they look if they are being visited in the ICU. I have noticed that people opt to tell lies instead of the truth because of the comfort they feel it will bring to the person they are lying to. People may have told you how nice you looked in a certain outfit, while telling others behind your back how tacky they really thought you looked. I am not dealing with whether these so called "little white lies" are right or wrong. I am only pointing this out as an example of how lying has been socialized into the social fabric of life itself. Others may refer to this as political correctness. Either way, it is intended to prevent others from feeling insulted, because sometimes the truth is not a very comforting thing to hear.

Although a lie is a lie no matter how little it may seem, I am more concerned about lies that are intended to disadvantage another for one's own benefit. I believe people tell lies for one of two reasons - to either make a gain or to avoid a pain. This can be accomplished by either withholding or falsifying information. When President Clinton confessed that he cheated on his wife and lied to her about it, I'm sure that was a painful confession. Maybe he was hoping to avoid the anticipated pain. A lie may seem more comforting when there is a threat of loss, but lying provides false comfort that will at some point become real hurt. When a negative ad is aimed at the character and reputation of a political candidate, the candidate to whom the ad was targeted usually counters with a subsequent ad disputing the validity of his or her opponent's claim. Who is telling the truth? Are both sides lying? Are political candidates being attacked, or are the minds of potential voters being attacked? One thing is for sure. Given enough time the true nature usually comes out. People have lied so much in politics that it seems to have become common place.

Maybe you do not relate to how withholding information or falsifying information in the political arena is lying. Maybe you need a more relevant scenario. Well, have you ever lied to a boyfriend, girlfriend, or spouse in order to avoid the consequences of what you did or did not do? Have you ever lied to your parents by not telling them the whole truth? Have you ever been under age and gone into a club, or bought alcohol with a fake I.D.? I am guilty even if you do not admit that you are too. Subsequently, I have learned that a lie is always laced with false comfort, which is different from discomfort. Discomfort is simply the absence of comfort, and sometimes we have to welcome the truth, even in the face of pain or loss.

We live in a world where we are almost forced to be crafty in how we present the truth the first time, if we want to have an opportunity to present the truth a second time. In the corporate world, references to your religious truth can be offensive to some. Many companies promote a healthy respect for other diversity dimensions such as race, ethnicity, gender, gender identity, age, sexual orientation, mental or physical ability, and national origin. All of these groups have their expectations of what is politically correct when you address them. Because of broad social injustices toward certain groups, one has to avoid unacceptable norms, especially in the area of religion and race. It is more comforting to be referred to as "African-American" as opposed to "that Negro" or as "Native American" instead of "those Indians." People do not want to be associated with language that implies or is a reference to injustice, disempowerment, or victimization. Whether political correctness or a little white lie, the noble idea is to avoid being offensive. Therefore, these concepts have been socialized into our world. Lying has become a part of the unwritten law of society, and we have to be careful not to become desensitized by the evil nature of lies.

How to Deal With a Liar

Over the years many people have come to me with relationship problems. I have realized that it is hard for people to discern the game when they are emotional and hurting. But, as a person on the outside looking in, it is easy for me to listen and apply the truth to a situation because I do not have the hurt, the pain, and the emotional interference. This is why I believe lawyers, PhD's, and even counselors have at points come to me for counsel. I am able to give sound advice because I did not have on the mental and emotional blinders. I credit this clarity mainly to my position. It is as if I'm looking at the same relationship landscape as they are, but from a higher point on the mountain. That is exactly what my new approach will do for those who embrace it. You will be able to separate yourself from the "low level of thinking" that interferes with your ability to discern the game because you have moved up on the mountain top.

Everyone is born with something called intuition. I believe it is a God given perception of truth that sounds an internal alarm whenever truth is threatened, much like the instinctive nature of animals. Although intuition is not infallible, it can serve as a natural trigger to move from instinct to a more deliberate assessment of a situation. According to infidelityman.com, an astonishing 70 percent of adultery victims are women. A survey by MSNBC revealed that 28 percent of married men have cheated on their partner. Of these cheaters only 2 percent have been caught by their partners, with 60 percent believing they totally got away undetected. Nearly 50 percent of men overall admit to being unfaithful at some time in their lives. The statistics on infidelity provide evidence that people have learned to lie very well. Here is a quick and easy four step exercise that I practice in my relationships when I have an intuitive suspicion that someone is lying.

1. ***Do not challenge the liar head on.*** The average liar has already practiced what to say to get out of a lie. This is where I have seen many women go wrong. They may say something like, *"I know you are lying. Where were you last night? We were supposed to have dinner and a movie! I called all over town looking for you! Did you forget or something?"* The guy then responds with something like this, *"Oh yeah, I did forget, I'm so sorry. I was at Joe's house playing pool; it must have slipped my mind."* So the woman challenges the lie by saying, *"I know you were not at Joe's*

house because that was one of the places I called, so where were you really?" The guy then gets defensive, *"What do you mean you called? Are you saying you don't trust me or something?"*
One lie necessitates another as they go round and round until the whole ordeal escalates into a more violent and abusive dialog. It is really a waste of your time to challenge a liar head on. All it will do is make the liar that much more cautious when playing relationship games with you in the future.

2. ***Allow the liar to tell as many lies as possible.*** You may have heard the cliché that the devil is in the details. Well, when it comes to lies, you should take that statement literally, because Satan has been hailed as the father of lies. The new living translation of John 8:44 says, "He was a murderer from the beginning and has always hated the truth. There is no truth in him. When Satan lies, it is consistent with his character; for he is a liar and the father of lies." This is another contrast between Satan, the enemy of God, and Jesus, the son of God. Jesus said to the accusers of his day in John 8:45,

"So when I tell the truth, you just naturally do not believe me!" Wow! That is why I have stated that one can become desensitized to the evil nature of a lie. No one could truthfully accuse Jesus of anything wrong; yet, they did not believe him because the truth wasn't in their nature anymore. It was as if lies were so common that no man could possibly be so squeaky clean. So I believe that when it comes to the truth, the Spirit of good is in the details, but when it comes to a destructive and deceptive lie, the spirit of evil is in the details. So, let the liar tell the lie and the more details you can get the better. The prior conversation may sound more like this. She asks, *"Where were you last night?"* He responds, *"Joe and I were playing pool at his house."* She continues to ask, *"Did you forget we were supposed to do dinner and a movie last night?"* He continues to respond, *"Oh yeah, it must have slipped my mind. I'm sorry; let me make it up to you."* At this point do not tell him that you called Joe's house and discovered he was not there! The idea is to continue to ask non-threatening follow-up questions such as, *"Were there any other guys there, or was it just you and Joe? Or, who won?"* You get the picture? Just gather as many false details as possible; say "ok"; and wait a while, which leads to the next step in this exercise.

3. ***Give the lie enough time to be forgotten.*** Yes, when you do not challenge the suspected lie head on, the liar will assume you believed it and forget about it. This is so effective that even if you are planning to use these tips to become a better liar, you will not be successful, because as a liar you will never see it coming.
4. ***After you have let some time go by, bring it back up again.*** For example, on the next time you schedule dinner and a movie, you can remind them not to forget like last time. Maybe that statement would be a good segue to ask, *"Why did you say you forgot last time?"* The response might be, *"Uhhh, well I don't know, I probably was playing basketball or something and lost track of time..."* The bottom line is that over a short period of time you are making a wise assessment of whether that

person is trustworthy. You will remember if the person's answers are not consistent when you ask the same questions again later. What you want to do is confirm your intuition that their stories never seem to add up. The person will not remember these things anyway, because it is hard to remember what did not really happen. But remember, you are not challenging the lie. You are just making an assessment of whether this person values the truth, because without truth, your relationship will fail. This wise assessment should come way before you get into a serious relationship with someone. Unfortunately, people are getting into relationships with people they can't trust quite often.

One of my favorite quotes is, "But wisdom is shown to be right by what results from it."[9] Based on that quote, let's revisit a few more statistical results of today's relationships, and you tell me if conventional wisdom has shown itself to be right.

- *People are imprisoned for murdering their partners.*[10]

- *Every other marriage in the modern western world ends in divorce.*
- *Two-million women per year, in intimate relationships, sustain injuries.*
- *Over a thousand women per year are murdered by their husbands or boyfriends.*

Those kinds of results lead me to believe that most relationships are not based on the wisdom of God, because God is not a fifty-fifty God. These statistics alone should tell us that something is not right. The culture of the game pushes against Godly wisdom like a magnetic repulsion. If we are going to beat the odds and have a successful relationship, we have to denounce the game altogether.

Bite Size

- When you understand that lying is the source of the game, you can then see why the game is inevitably going to come your way. Many of us can relate to the fact that we live in a world where people tell lies.
- The more we become desensitized to lies, the more they will become a part of our nature, and once lying has become a part of our nature, it will becomes a part of our character as a person.
- Truth is radically different from a lie and is the opposing force that must be used to combat lying.
- Truth sets us apart from what opposes it, which is anything that is based on a lie.
- Once you start to value the truth, it will become a part of your good nature, and you will push away from anything that is based on a lie, a sort of spiritual magnetic repulsion.
- Lying has become a part of the unwritten law of society, and we have to be careful not to become desensitized by the evil nature of lies.

Chapter 4

THE PROCESS OF THE GAME

Soft and Soothing

As we continue with the true story of the college couple I am calling Fred and Wilma, they are now very much into an exclusive relationship. We now understand that Fred is a very popular fraternity guy, is an athlete, and has a relatively nice car. Fred is one year ahead of Wilma in college, and when he is around the guys, his personal fulfillment objective is admittedly sexual. Wilma, on the other hand, has quietly traded sex for financial support, transportation and social status. It has now been several months, and the spring semester is coming to a close. Both Fred and Wilma are satisfied with what they are getting out of the relationship. In preparation to leave, Fred manages to set-up a series of sexual escapades throughout the weeks, days, and nights before they break for summer.

Fred helps Wilma load her things into the trunk of his car the morning she is scheduled to fly home to Chicago. He drops her off at the airport where they both express intense feelings of infatuation, hoping it will preserve the relationship until they return for the fall semester. A series of amorous phone calls and text messaging is their plan to keep the fire burning over the summer. Wilma quickly sets the stage as her flight is called for boarding. "Fred, I'm going to miss you so much. I don't know what I'm going to do without you this summer." Fred replies, "Me neither, I'm missing you already! I've got to find a way to see you at least once this summer." I know says Wilma, "You've better make sure you keep all the girls at bay, I don't want anybody trying to steal my man." Fred offers another comforting hug as he says, "You don't have anything to worry about; **you are the only person I want to be with***."*

Of course they kiss and grope for reassurance, as these words are all they have to carry them through a summer of sexual cold turkey each assumes the other has agreed upon. Fred knows he must live up to this perception of being sexless over the summer, so that he can continue what he started when they return for the fall semester. Wilma sees the temporary celibacy as a way to honor their exclusive commitment recently made to one another. Fred waves goodbye and drives himself home to a nearby city not far from campus.

The process of the game is very simple, yet profound, because it can take different paths. Basically, it starts with persuasive communication. The persuasive part of the game is what I call the soft and soothing, easy feel good part of the game. This is what happened when Fred first met Wilma, and they both put their best foot forward in how they looked, talked, smelled, etc. The more they appeared perfect to one another, the more eager they became to crack the euphoric shell, and experience the rush of what was perceived to be waiting inside. When Fred said that Wilma was "**the only person he wanted to be with**," he was using a classic persuasive tactic. Typically, when a promise is kept or perception of reward is received, this can be a legitimate use of persuasion, but when promises are broken and the perceived reward is lost, persuasion can be perceived as nothing more than a conning, lying, cheating, you no what. Remember, the mind is the battlefield; therefore the goal of a player is to influence the thoughts of another so the person will do or agree to something that the player wants. You can imagine how crazy this can become when all parties involved are playing games.

Persuasive communication has been around since the beginning of time. It was used by Satan in Genesis chapter three to deceive Eve into eating from the tree of the knowledge of good and evil.[11] Verse six details how Eve was persuaded by the thought that eating fruit from the forbidden tree was not only good for food, but was pleasant to the eyes, but so were all the other trees according to Genesis chapter two verse nine. The only distinct temptation was the idea that the fruit would make one wise. The irony is that the wisdom was not in eating the fruit, but rather in obeying God's command to not eat from the tree in the first place.[12] Consequently, both Adam and his wife's eyes were opened to the fact that they were walking around naked, so they made an attempt to cover and hide themselves from the presence of God. God asks Adam, "Have you eaten from the tree I commanded you not to eat?" Adam answered, "The woman gave it to me and I did eat."

Adam's answer sparked two funny thoughts in my mind. One thought is that man seems to have blamed the woman for his lack of leadership since the beginning of time. The other is that after Eve was persuaded to eat the forbidden fruit and gave some to Adam, it seems man has been seeking revenge against the woman ever since! As a man that may be a funny thought, but some women have suffered pain from men for so long that they are laughing only to keep from crying. People who play games are like serpents, especially men who target women they think are gullible or easy to persuade. I do not think the average woman is at all gullible. For the most part, when a woman has feelings and cares for a guy, she wants to trust him. However, her quick trigger to trust is what makes persuasion seem so easy. In my opinion, that is not being gullible, that is just a woman who prematurely thought she could trust a man. This can be avoided with the simple understanding that one can like a person he or she just met today, but trust has to be earned over time. If someone is trying really hard to win your trust, take a step back and ask yourself why. Is there something urgently needed or wanted from you? What is the personal fulfillment objective? Allow yourself enough time to discern why someone is so anxious to gain your trust.

Obviously gaining trust is a very important factor in the persuasive process. People who play relationship games do not mind putting in a certain amount of persuasive work upfront to get you to slack up on your defenses, because when you lower your defenses, it becomes easier and faster for your opponent to score. Eve's willingness to trust the serpent was accomplished in part by advocating a perceived reward, even the reward of being like God. It is interesting that the form of Satan is emphasized by the subtle character of a serpent. According to Revelation chapter twelve verse nine, Satan was once an angel of light, but became an enemy of God and was cast out of heaven, along with multitudes of others who became his angels of darkness. Satan was separated from God because of sin, although he was not stripped of his cunning and crafty ways. While waiting on the fate that he willed upon himself, Satan grew more desirous to destroy mankind; and the only way to accomplish that was to underhandedly separate man from God. Satan knew he had no power to physically wipe man from the face of the earth; therefore, he had to lure mankind into the same self-destructive pit of temptation, to touch, taste and experience the forbidden.

The Rush of the Forbidden

When I was a kid, my friends and I spent more time outside than we did inside. The video game consoles were not as consuming as they are today. We were forced to make up games and use our outdoor creativity to have fun. However, this often led to mischief as we found ourselves growing weary of the same old outdoor games. We had to come up with something more fun and exciting that would not wear off so quickly; something that would keep us coming back for more time and time again. In our quest for the ultimate outdoor experience, we discovered there was a great rush in activities of danger. We found that rush in things such as stealing grocery carts and racing them down the steepest hills we could find. We also achieved that rush as one person would stand and pedal a bicycle down a steep hill, while the other would ride on the handle bars; and another would ride the seat. On one instance, just before the hill was about to level out, the driver lost control of the bicycle and we all hit the pavement at what felt like 100 miles per hour. I still have the scars to show for it. We quickly realized that the danger was not worth it and came up with other ways to get the rush we wanted without killing ourselves.

It did not take us long to discover a rush that posed less danger. I do not know what this game is called, but we would take turns going up to a random house in the neighborhood to ring the doorbell, only to take off running for the nearest hiding place. As the resident opened the door he or she became suspicious that those darn kids were playing again. They would scream all kind of expletives preceding the words, "don't let me catch you on my porch again…" You can fill in the blank. For us it was the ultimate rush! Although temporary, our mood would drastically change from boring to exciting in a flash. Every new house we targeted solicited unique reactions, some of which we rated higher than others. It was as if we were becoming addicted to the mental sensation and the sheer feeling of doing something we clearly knew was forbidden. I have termed these types of experiences "the rush of the forbidden."

The rush we got from playing this childhood game is not much different from the rush people get today from the current dating culture. Many people get a rush from the idea of having different sex partners, being with someone else's spouse, or cheating on their own spouse. This can create a psychological addiction that is difficult to shake, as we long for an experience that is better than the one before. Even unprotected sex can be a rush. If you really listen and observe as I have, you will also conclude that we live in a culture that is continuously driven by the search for something better. A better dining experience, a better movie going experience, and even a better church-going experience; you name it and there is a longing for something better. Do not get me wrong; I'm all for better, as long as it maintains a sense of integrity toward certain spiritual and moral values. We have to be careful not to allow our longing for something better to get so out of control that it defeats the purpose. Without a spiritual and moral filter, longing for something better can cause one to slowly slip from the reality of what exists, to the fantasy of what does not exist.

Part of the allure of the tree of the knowledge of good and evil was stimulated by the rush of the forbidden. Eating the fruit was thought to make one like God. The same desire that caused Satan to fall from heaven was being used on earth to perpetuate the fall of man. As over indulgent humans socialized by a culture of what's next and what's better, we tend to want what we give our attention to the most. For example, as we start our morning radio show drives, pass our daily supermodel billboards, click on our office PCs, plug in our afternoon iPods, and repeat our evening commutes, multimedia will have bombarded most of our eyes and ears with repetitious cravings for something better. Just as the attention given to the forbidden fruit created a greater lust for the fruit, when we finally pull into the safety of our driveways, we have worked up more desperation for our nightly fix of sexy sitcoms that incite the forbidden fantasies for the things we know we can not realistically have.

Hard and Hurtful

Have you ever been in a relationship for a while that started going down hill but you did not know exactly why? If so, you have experienced the hard and hurtful process of evasion. Evasion is used when someone wants to get out of a perceived obligation without making good on the promise or reward. It means to avoid doing or fulfilling an obligation. It involves escaping a perceived obligation by use of trickery, slyness, secrecy and deception. Be careful when a person says, "**You are the only person I want to be with**". If your hand is not being asked in marriage, it probably means you are the only person I want to be with right now. Later on there could be two, three, four or many more people sharing in the relationship, because now and later are two different points in time. When a relationship gets to the evasive part of the process, someone has already turned heartless, and it is usually the guy. Let's take a final look at what happened over the summer as Fred and Wilma are now back together on campus for the fall semester.

It is a beautiful fall day on campus as Wilma reunites with Fred ready to pick up where they left off last semester. Over the summer, Wilma initiated most of the phone calls and text messages that sustained the relationship and kept the fire burning. There were times when Wilma wondered why Fred couldn't call her between breaks and lunches on his "night job". Fred would explain how his supervisor strictly enforced fifteen minute breaks and thirty minute lunches. He also made up the lie that cell phone usage was limited to emergencies during work hours. There was just no time to make phone calls because he worked so hard each summer to pay his way through school. Although Wilma was suspicious, she was convinced that Fred would not lie to her. Truthfully, Fred worked a very flexible day job and made sure he returned Wilma's calls not only at breaks and lunches during the day, but several times throughout his regular work day to cover up for his fictitious night job. The truth is that Fred secretly spent most of his nights transferring his emotions from Wilma to the new love of his life. Ladies, herein is why the evasive process is so hard and hurtful.

First, women must understand that when a player begins the process of evasion, he has also started transferring his emotions to another woman long before the evasive process is over. When Wilma was feeling suspicious over the summer, the transfer was taking place then, maybe even sooner. During the following semester, Wilma continued to be suspicious and wondered why Fred was so distant. Fred began frequent trips home on the weekends without Wilma, claiming to have weekend work opportunities. Obviously, Fred was working on a sexual and emotional relationship with another female. For months and even years some women are just unable to put their finger on it. Many women know something is not right, but are blinded by their own emotional investment in the relationship.

Second, at the point a man is ready to end the relationship; he has pretty much emptied out his emotions and feelings for you and has transferred them to another relationship. Unfortunately, in Wilma's case, she ignored her intuition and hung on to her hope for a successful relationship. Fred the player was very ok with the state of the relationship since his personal fulfillment objective was purely sexual. He dragged Wilma along, while he continued to transfer emotionally to the other woman. From time to time, Fred would bait Wilma with the right words simply to prolong his sexual objective. The proverbial emotional rollercoaster ride took a tremendous toll on Wilma before she finally accepted that something was not right with the relationship. At this point, Wilma decides to do something she should have been doing all along. She decides to communicate.

"Fred, you are graduating this semester and we have not talked about our relationship going forward." Fred replies, *"What is there to talk about? All we have done is*

fuss and fight this entire year." Wilma responds, *"So that's all you have to say about us; how do you feel about me?"* Fred answers, *"I've been thinking about this for a while, and I don't want to have a long distance relationship."* Wilma responds, *"I don't either that's why I was planning to move in with you after I graduate." "You don't understand," Fred replies, "I don't think we need to see each other anymore. I mean you have another year left in college, and I don't see how it is going to work."* Wilma's heart drops as she exclaims outrageously: *"So it sounds like you're just giving up on the relationship after all we've been through, how could you be so cold?"* Fred blasts back, *"I'm not cold I'm just being real! We don't really have a good relationship anyway!"* Although it sounds like it is over, it is never over until the painful finish. How would it make you feel if this was your relationship? Here are a few things that happened to Wilma and others like her who have experienced this hard and hurtful evasive process.

- Although physical brokenness is not excluded, many women are left emotionally broken. Some feel gutted and hollow inside and try to fill that emptiness by sleeping around promiscuously. The guy in this case is empty only because he has transferred to another woman emotionally, but the female is empty because she has a surplus of emotions that have no specific object of affection anymore. Her emptiness is sandwiched between desertion and betrayal.

- Some women turn cold and develop a callous heart with little desire to be touched by a man, because they do not want to feel that way ever again. The process is just too hard and hurtful of a process to repeat.
- Some women who are given just a tainted form of affection will give in because it makes them feel good for the moment. They are so tired of feeling the pain that they are willing to sacrifice anything just for the moment. They long for the soft and soothing, the easy feel good part of the game, and end up in an endless cycle of persuasion and evasion.

Usually, the man tends to be the victimizer more often than the women. Most victimizers do not want to face their victim. This is why many guys will secretly transfer emotionally. They do not want to deal with the consequences of their actions. They have no desire to be accountable to the victim. And they are too weak to handle the emotional break up. They are living such a lie that it can not be explained anyway; therefore, they choose to evade without the woman knowing. It is the easy, cowardly way out- the path of least resistance.

Of course, not everyone intentionally looks to get caught up in the game, but if you continue to play games, eventually this type of hurt has a way of playing out in your relationship. No matter how street smart you are; no matter how much experience you have in life; no matter how sophisticated you think you are; if you go into relationships playing games, this type of hurt will find you, and I promise you will not see it coming because it is all based on a lie.

Nuts and Bolts

When I was a small boy I would help my dad work on car engines. I remember him struggling at times to loosen a nut from the engine block while simultaneously holding a flashlight. He would shout for me, and I would come running to save the day. “Hold this flashlight,” he would say. It did not seem like an important job at the time, but now that I have a small son of my own, I understand how helpful holding a flashlight can be. My dad’s old car had old nuts that required the combined grease from both his old elbows to loosen those old bolts. My old man not only taught me a lesson about auto mechanics, but now, I’m able to relate his lessons to relationships.

The persuasive process is the easy feel good part of the game. Everything feels fresh and inviting like a brand new curvy red corvette on the showroom floor with its hood up, quietly whispering, “Check me out.” The power house engine block contains the cylinders and their components inside a cooled and lubricated crankshaft, which typically comprises the largest physical cavity of the engine. There are no spots or blemishes, as this car is flawlessly polished to perfection. And the shiny new bolts penetrating the corresponding nuts are not hindered by rust, but the right amount of lubricant makes them very easy to screw. Go ahead and visualize the male in the relationship as a six inch bolt, and the corresponding female as the nut. No offense ladies, I'm just trying to drive my point home so that you can really see the painful finish for what it is.

We will let the engine block represent your heart. If either is broken it must be repaired in order for everything else to function. The newness of a relationship can feel as good as or better than a brand new car, but eventually, newness will wear off. A woman's make-up will not always be flawless. At some point it will wear off like a bad paint job in desperate need of a touch up. Most men need extensive body work as we get older, so we work out. Bad hair days will sometimes become covered with a weave, baseball cap, wig, toupee or hairpiece. Both of you will need something more to maintain your interest as you grow familiar with each other over time. Interest can only be sustained when two people connect spiritually. Otherwise no matter how much you dress yourselves up, these old familiar glimpses of reality will activate a super power that neither of you knew you had. He will no longer see the beautiful dress you are wearing, because his x-ray vision allows him to see the body shaper that is holding your stomach in. She will no longer enjoy the designer fragrance that originally attracted her to you, because her super senses have become so familiar with your true body odor that the cologne does not mask it anymore. All of the things that drew you to each other have started to get old, just like the paint job on that little red corvette. The nuts and bolts are starting to get loose causing things to sag out of place. You've screwed as much as you can to keep it together but you just can't get it tight enough. Consequently, his attention now turns to the newer cars that are displayed on the showroom floors. He begins contemplating how to trade you in for the newer, younger, sleeker model. This type of temporary interest can be found when the only connection two people had was physical.

Players are always at the dealership test driving and negotiating until a deal can be made. Some people know that they will be traded in; others simple get kicked to the curb. Even for a car, this type of evasion is not over until it gets crushed. Often, when the relationship is ending, some of the truth will start to come out. And the truth will hurt, not because it is true but because you have wasted so much time and invested so much emotional energy into a deceptive relationship. The evasive process always leads to an unhappy ending, but it is never over until the painful finish. It is like the grand finale of a Fourth of July fireworks display; the sparks will fly, but the heavy artillery is usually what ends the show. Here is what happens in the final stages of the evasive process.

1. **Carelessness:** This is the point in the game when one of the two wants out of the relationship but has not communicated it to the other person involved. Usually it is the guy who has totally separated himself emotionally and is well on his way to transferring his emotions to another relationship. The transfer happens while the relationship is still in tact, but once the transfer is complete, you will find out about discontent, infidelities, addictions, anger problems, streaks of violence, and other well kept secrets because the person simply does not care anymore. He wants out and knows that carelessness will make you more willing to let him go without clinging on. The unfortunate reality is that some women stay in hopeless relationships, because they do not know how to let go. After all, she did not transfer her emotions to someone else

like he did. Carelessness is like a can of WD-40 that is sprayed on an old rusty nut and bolt relationship only to loosen things up. This is not likely where the relationship will end because the average woman has too many unanswered questions for it to end here. Some women allow men to drag them down to absolutely nothing, just so they can find out why.

2. **Drama:** Asking the why question to a person who no longer cares leads to the next stage of this hard and hurtful process. The relationship becomes very dramatic and eventually becomes public information. No place is off limits for an argument or fight to break out. Everyone who did not see the drama will eventually hear about your problems through word of mouth. She begins to demand the truth even though she knows it will be painful. The little red corvette is in full throttle as her engine block is dangerously bleeding oil. The carelessness and drama has driven her into the ground, and now she finally wants out. All of the carelessness and drama has loosened what used to be a tight nut and

bolt relationship, and now it is getting close to the end. Yet, even though the old nut and bolt is loose, it still takes time to screw it off. Relationships that have much invested are hard for a woman to end without knowing why. She uses the last bit of fuel left to scream out a litany of questions: *"you told me you loved me! How could you do this to me after all I've done for you? Who do you think you are? Why did I even waste my time with you?"* The nut and bolt is finally on edge, very close to being screwed off, but it is not over until the painful finish.

3. **The Painful finish:** This stage of the game happens when someone wants out so badly that he or she would do almost anything to end the relationship, but the other person is not ready to let go just yet. The person being left with all the emotional pain can feel so much rejection that he or she loses all sense of self and makes one final attempt to hold on to someone who does not want to hold on to him or her. The big fireworks explosion that many have come to know as the

grand finale is about to end the show. Violence, abuse and character assassination at its worst will probably happen in this stage of the relationship. This is when what was once seen as love turns into war. It is no longer about you anymore. It's about you won't leave me alone, so now I have to push you, beat you, slap you, do whatever is necessary to get you to wake-up to the reality that it is over! You finally get closure when he talks about the things he knows you can't easily change. After all, the "can of carelessness" is empty. He begins his explosive finish by answering your questions with the most painful remarks imaginable. *"You are too old and short, and I can't stand your family! You need to lose some weight; I was only with you for the sex from the beginning! I don't want you anymore! I wish you would just leave me alone!"*

Unfortunately, this is the point where many people will find time to take the concepts in this book seriously. Over the years, as I have shared this information in seminars, many have come to realize that the game really has been their enemy all along. One of the points I want to get through to you is that no one can live up to the self-image of society, because it is not real! That is why you must denounce the fantasy of the game and embrace people who appreciate the reality of who you are. **You are a treasure waiting to be found**.

Have you ever been through something like this? If so, do you want to continue experiencing that process? Are you ready to denounce, discern and dodge the game altogether? I encourage you to commit my 3D view to memory, so that you can avoid the emotional and sexual drama that is involved in the culture of the game. The baggage of issues we pack from playing relationship games usually ends up getting unloaded on the one who really doesn't deserve it. Often, we do not know how deeply affected we are by these past experiences until they are unpacked in our marriage relationships. It is in marriage where we spend much of our time digging and weeding, instead of planting and reaping. Here again is why divorce is so rampant. Do not let the culture of the game rob you of your successful Garden of Eden relationship. The Game has always been one big lie. Denounce it, discern it, and Dodge it from here on out.

Bite Size

- The process of the game starts with soft and soothing, easy feel good, persuasive communication.
- The goal of a player is to influence the thoughts of another so that person will do or agree to something that the player wants.
- Gaining trust is a very important factor in the persuasive process. People who play relationship games do not mind putting in a certain amount of persuasive work upfront to get you to slack up on your defenses.
- The process of the game ends with hard and hurtful evasive communication.
- Evasion is used when someone wants to get out of a perceived obligation without making good on the promise or reward.
- At the time a man begins to evade, he is very close to having emptied out his emotions and feelings for you and has transferred them to another relationship.

Chapter 5

THE POWER TO IMPROVE

The Results of Wisdom

If the men of our society would embrace the concepts of this book, I believe the woman would find it a relief to encounter such a specimen, because as men we have a tremendous power to improve on whatever we are given. Improve means to increase the value of something by making it better, more desirable, or bringing it to a more excellent condition. I am a firm believer that the man should use his power to improve the spiritual, emotional, mental, physical, and financial condition of the woman. At the time this book was written, the Supreme Court, which is the highest judicial body in the US, was represented by only two female justices of the nine. Of the four hundred thirty-five house representatives that make up the US Congress, only seventy-four were female. Out of one-hundred senators, only sixteen were female. Of all the top five-hundred publicly traded companies, only thirteen had female CEOs. Men continue to dominate the entertainment industry and almost every other commercial enterprise. I'm only mentioning this to reinforce what I believe is a God-given power to lead. If we really stop and think about the tremendous influence men have, we can conclude that the world will either get better or worse because of our leadership.

When reading the Declaration of Independence, it is evident that the founding fathers were influenced by a belief in God. The well-known second sentence reads, "We hold these truths to be self-evident, that all men are created equal, that they are endowed by their Creator with certain unalienable rights, that among these are Life, Liberty and the pursuit of Happiness." Thomas Jefferson, the principal drafter of the Declaration, acknowledged a belief in God on November 29, 1775 as follows: *"Believe me, dear Sir: there is not in the British Empire a man who more cordially loves a union with Great Britain than I do. But, by the God that made me, I will cease to exist before I yield to a connection on such terms as the British Parliament propose; and in this, I think I speak the sentiments of America."*[13]

The final section of the Declaration appeals to the Supreme judge of the world for the "rectitude of the

Framer's intentions." In other words, the Framers were concerned about moral virtue, religious correctness, and the quality of being upright. With emphasis on the words "Creator" and the name "God" as referenced by Jefferson, I believe America has always had a conscience towards God that was crucial to preserving the moral good over the past two-hundred years. Much of the wisdom that supports the phrase "one Nation under God," four words from the thirty-one word pledge of allegiance, is a result of biblical wisdom that the founding fathers possessed. Again, I believe wisdom is shown to be right by what results from it. Therefore, it is vitally important to at least acknowledge the biblical influence that helped shape the conscience of America.

In 1982 Newsweek published a cover story which stated, *"For centuries the Bible has exerted an unrivaled influence on American culture, politics, and social life. Now historians are discovering that the Bible, perhaps even more than the Constitution, is our founding document.*[13]*"* Political philosophy professors Donald Lutz and Charles Hyneman researched the sources most often referenced in our nation's founding documents. After reviewing an estimated fifteen thousand items, their findings revealed that the Bible, especially the book of Deuteronomy, contributed thirty-four percent of all quotations used by our Founding Fathers. [13]

What Do You Believe?

What you say and do can give insight into whether you are influenced by the self-image of society or have a firm set of personal beliefs. For example, do you tend to be more comfortable with publically acknowledging the universe instead of God, even though you privately profess Christianity? Or, are you more comfortable with relegating religious matters to nature? There are a collection of politically correct things to do and say that are likely the spawn of a noble desire to avoid offending society, while we secretly insult our own personal belief system. What's popular continues to modify social perceptions and provides a framework for generating, sustaining, and applying those perceptions. For instance, the use of language such as "Godspeed" sounds more like a catchphrase than a belief. Godspeed is a phrase meaning "God prosper you." But so does the phrase "God bless you." It means "empowered to prosper" as used in several King James Bible verses.

Genesis 1:26-28 reads, *"And God said, Let us make man in our image, after our likeness: and let them have dominion over the fish of the sea, and over the fowl of the air, and over the cattle, and over all the earth, and over every creeping thing that creepeth upon the earth.* ***27*** *So God created man in his own image, in the image of God created he him; male and female created he them.* ***28*** *And God* ***blessed*** *them, and God said unto them, be fruitful, and multiply, and replenish the earth, and subdue it:"* Notice, God blessed, or empowered to prosper, in verse twenty-eight, but more importantly in verse twenty-six, God empowered "them," the male and the female, to have dominion together. Instead, some men seem to embrace the opposing idea that the male should dominate the female. Everything God gave man in the Garden of Eden, including the very first woman, was given to man to improve upon.

The Word in Genesis also tells us to be fruitful, multiply, replenish the earth, and subdue it. All four of those words have something very special in common; they improve life. To be fruitful is to be highly productive with the seed we have been given. When you multiply something good the result is something better. Everything on this earth has come to exist because of multiplication. Replenish means to make full and complete what was once void. I am sure you can see how replenishing has led to something better. What was once empty has been made full and now has meaning. Together, man and woman are to subdue the earth, bringing under control anything that tries to stop this process of improvement. As men we are born to lead, but we can not do it without the woman.

The question then becomes, are we improving a woman's life, or are we making her life worse? When a woman leaves your presence, is she better off having encountered you or does she need to be renovated like a condemned building? When you speak to women do you speak life words or death words to her? For instance, when she does not fall for your pick-up lines, do you call her a b!+@#, whore, slut, or tramp? Those are words that speak death to a woman's soul. Men are supposed to add to a woman, not take away from her. When a woman comes into your presence she should leave improved, even if she is not the one for you. Do not take away from her and devalue the essence of her beauty. Help preserve the treasure that God has designated her to be for someone else. That understanding alone will go a long way in transforming your relationships.

So the question still remains "what do you believe?" Do you believe fragments of worldviews offered by various belief systems depending on the situation you are in? Or, have you been endowed by God your Creator, with certain unalienable rights? Genesis 2:7 says, "And the LORD God formed man of the dust of the ground, and breathed into his nostrils the breath of life; and man became a living soul." I would be remiss if I did not answer this question myself. I believe my right to life and liberty came through the gift of Christ.[14] I believe my liberty is accomplished in his mission.[15] And I believe my happiness is in the wisdom and understanding of His words.[16] The universe is vast and flawless; the stars are numerous and orderly; there's rapid motion in the sea, yet there is balance, and all this, I believe, is by the wisdom of God. What do you believe?

Where Are You?

Several other interesting questions are asked in Genesis, but in Chapter three and verse nine, God asks a question that not only Adam struggled to answer, but every man thereafter has struggled with as well. Men have always struggled with the question, "Where are you?" From the time we were children, a woman has inquired about our geographical position as we became more eager to explore the world around us. As teenage boys, we all longed for that day of freedom where curfew was no longer enforced. And wasn't it more often than not a woman's voice restricting our freedom? The very freedom we all longed for when we were children has become the freedom we fear losing as adults.

When Eve ate the forbidden fruit and offered it to Adam almost brandishing the fact that she did not drop dead, that helped persuade Adam to eat it himself. How often have we taken a chance because someone else impressed upon us that there was no harm and no foul involved? Maybe the lie is that we won't get caught or it will be our little secret. No matter how secluded and private your geographical location may be, it will never exempt you from answering the question, "Where are you?" As a believer, "where you are" is not a question of geographical location, but a question of spiritual position of authority and leadership. What you believe is what determines where you are. As a leader in corporate America for over 18 years, I was often asked the question, "Where are you on this issue?" My response was not, "I'm right here on that issue." My response was based on what I believe! Likewise, God, who gave instructions to Adam before hand, was questioning Adam's position of leadership. Adam's response was similar to the average man's response today. When men are caught in a wrongful act, in essence we are caught out of position. And when the act is over, just like children, our first response is to hide.

As men, we can not put our trust in will power, especially when a desirable woman is involved, because as soon as our will betrays us, our instinct is to hide. You may think you will only allow yourself to go so far, but you can not rely on will power alone. You will find yourself going a little bit further each time, until you have done what you thought you would not do. God's desire is for mankind to dominate and never to hide from any situation, but His intent was never for us to have dominion through will-power. Adam and Eve were both put in position by God to dominate because they had a spiritual connection with God. Ultimately, both Adam and Eve lost sight of their position, but notice the question, "where are you?" was asked only to Adam. It was the man who was held responsible for not walking in his position of leadership and authority, not the woman.

As men of today, "where are you?" is still a valid question. Adam was the first to be created, and by virtue of that fact, God expected him to be the first line of spiritual instruction, vision, and communication. This lack of leadership in the first man continues to be avoided by mankind today. What a sobering question when we look at it in this context. We do not know what would have been the outlook of mankind had Adam obeyed because there still would have been the consequences of Eve's disobedience. What we do know is the end result of both their actions was charged to man's account. After both man and woman had experienced the rush of the forbidden, they were able to feel something they had never before been conscious of, the knowledge of good and evil. They only knew happiness prior to that rush, but now they were able to experience sadness. They were naked and unashamed prior to that rush, but now it was as if they were stripped of their armor and exposed to the enemy. They were once in unity with God prior to that rush, but now they were separated and needed to be restored. As the rush of the forbidden continued to entice, they were persuaded that there was no harm and no foul, but once the act was over, they could see how deceived they really were in eating the forbidden fruit. When they partook of the forbidden fruit the time bomb of death started ticking not only for them, but all of mankind. No, they did not die immediately, but Adam and Eve were both kicked out of the garden no longer having access to the tree of life that would have caused them to live forever. The statement "You will not surely die" was a lie, and over time Adam and Eve both died in more ways than one, just as God warned they would.

The evil nature of a lie that crept into Adam and Eve's relationship is still happening in our relationships today. The culture of the game is a hard and hurtful process that is based on such lies. Satan is the father of lies, and he plants them in an effort to steal, kill and destroy. We may not see the immediate effects of physical death in our life, but just as Fred and Wilma, we know this emotional, social, financial and spiritual death all too well. Many of us spent our youth playing games and now we are over thirty and want a serious relationship. That can feel like death when you look around and it seems like there is no hope for you. It can feel like death when you have lost valuable time, money, and the ability to let another person into your heart again. It can feel like death if you started out giving your trust away freely, but now you are afraid to trust anyone. No you have not yet died physically, but to resuscitate your soul and bring back the pure radiance that once was is a draining process that only God can restore.

Moreover, the eyes of Adam and Eve's conscience were opened. It had to be in order for them to experience the joy of good and the guilt of evil. The only thing they gained from the rush of the forbidden was a low level of knowledge that we all experience today-- an endless war against the knowledge of good and evil. The law of our mind was completely good, but now the law that dwells in our body is awakened and wants to hold us captive to the evil nature that can only be overcome with good. One man who failed to answer the question, "where are you?" passed on this internal war against good and evil to all of mankind.[17] Adam and his wife initiated these unfortunate results all because they believed the lie that "you will not surely die." Death is one of our many enemies on this earth, but according to God, death is the last enemy that will be swallowed up in victory.[18] I hope you are getting this truth that the culture of the game embodies this same evil nature of lies, and without lies the game would not exist.

Call of Duty

As men and women, we all engage in spiritual warfare, even if one is an atheist. Not only do we war within ourselves, but we war outside of ourselves as well. We know now that the question "where are you?" is not one of geographical location, but one of position, authority, leadership, and power that comes from standing for God. We know that our struggle is not with a flesh and blood opponent. Every day we encounter some level of resistance in this world without moving a finger. We either encounter this resistance in our homes, on our jobs, in business, school or wherever there is an official structure of rulers, authorities, powers, and spiritual forces of evil that exist. Although the people in power can be challenged, the right to exercise that power will continue to exist until the ALL POWERFUL GOD of heaven returns to set the record straight. So, as Christians it is our duty to be constant in our faith, both in season and out of season, always remaining conscious of spiritual wickedness in high places, making sure that we fight within the law of the land. If you are against abortion, for instance, find a legal way to advocate for life; do not blow up an abortion clinic! That is not Christianity! The good fight of faith must be fought within the law of the land. One can not walk in faith if he does not value the truth. And how you answer the question "where are you?" will either position you for the call of duty or place you red-handed at the scene of the crime.

I know now that the culture of the game has always existed, but the devastating progression is that as time goes on, its players and victims are getting younger and younger. Maybe it is because parents do not have time to parent anymore. Data from the 2000 administration of National

Assessment of Educational Progress showed that among eighth graders, only 57 percent of parents participated in parent-teacher conferences. According to the Southwest Educational Development Laboratory, a combination of research on parent involvement over the past decade concluded that regardless of family income or background, students with involved parents are more likely to succeed educationally, socially and behaviorally. Many parents are preoccupied with work and often leave their children vulnerable to mass media influence and negative peer pressure. Others are single mothers where the father is typically not very much involved. I encourage every man to spend time with your kids as much as your situation will allow. Spending quality time may be difficult, but as parents who care we can either raise our kids now or attempt to raise them later in their adult lives. No matter where we are in our parent-child relationship, parenting is our duty, and we must accept the call.

What I've learned over the years is that God directs my steps not my sitting. As I have acted on the things I know to do, my steps have been directed toward the things I did not know to do. Many people are sitting on the couch right now believing that something miraculous will happen to them, but are doing absolutely nothing within their power. Every place in the bible where a reward is promised, we must do something that is well within our power in order to receive it. For example, God is not dropping money out of the sky; that would make God a counterfeiter and we've already said that as Christians we must operate within the law of the land. When God blesses you financially it will be amazing, but not necessarily miraculous. In other words, you will know exactly how you received certain blessings. Even if you do not know why someone gave you something, you do know that someone gave you something.

In the book of Luke chapter six, it talks about our duty to God and man. We are instructed not to judge one another or condemn others, to give and to forgive; but in verse 38 it says, "Give, and it shall be given unto you; good measure, pressed down, and shaken together, and running over, shall men give into your bosom." The New Living Translation of this verse says, "Whatever measure you use in giving – large or small – it will be used to measure what is given back to you." We read here that giving to others is well within our power, whether large or small; therefore, receiving from others is the promise of reward, which is the byproduct of giving within your power. If someone gave you your dream car you would know exactly how you received that car. God did not drop the car out of the sky. If He did there would be no vehicle identification number, no taxes paid, the car would not even be registered with the department of motor vehicles. That would be a miracle! God always does things decently and in order, so when it comes to material blessings God is very legalistic. We should be careful not to confuse material blessings with spiritual blessings such as divine healing, which can happen miraculously.

It is very important that Christians sincerely answer to the true calling of God's word, and not become pacified by the privilege of being rewarded. I am very careful about the church I attend and the pastor I open myself to. Organized church worship and teaching for the most part is a place where people come to receive spiritual food for healthy spiritual growth, to equip us to continue the works of Christ until He returns. It is our duty as parishioners to seek the practical knowledge of Christ and not just religious formality or performances. Isaiah 53:11 says,

"…by the knowledge of him (Christ) shall my righteous servant justify many." Many churches have resorted to religious stunts to attract people and have lost focus of the knowledge that Christ says, "if I be lifted up I will draw all men unto me."[19] Instead, people are often lifted up above others, when the truth is that every person is small enough to be found in Christ. Isn't that partly what separates the kingdom of God from the culture of the game? Does God really choose the people that this culture overlooks to confound the wise and shame the strong? Or, has the corrupt culture of the game crept into the church? Are we really pressing toward the mark, the prize of the high calling of God in Christ Jesus? Is it not our duty to seek God for our true calling and walk in it so that our gift can truly make room for us?

Of course I could go on for several more paragraphs about our duty as Christians on a broader scale, but my focus is on the culture of the game and how we can positively affect change. Therefore, I will leave you with one additional duty that I believe we should start with in order to answer the ultimate call, which is to dwell together in unity. Then we will have done our part to position ourselves where God has commanded the blessings to flow in a place where we can receive the blessings; but as long as we are selfishly disjointed, the church will always be a figurative body of believers operating with limitations.[20]

Bite Size

- Everything God gave man in the Garden of Eden, including the very first woman, was given to man to improve upon.
- Man should use his power to improve the spiritual, emotional, mental, physical and financial condition of the woman.
- When a woman comes into your presence she should leave improved, even if she is not the one for you.
- Men stay involved with your kids; we have a tremendous power to improve on whatever we are given.
- No matter where you are in your parent-child relationship, parenting is your duty and you must accept the call.
- God's desire is for man and woman to have dominion over this earth together and never hide from any situation, but His intent was never for man to dominate the woman.

- As Christians, it is our duty to remain constant in faith and fight within the law of the land.
- It is our duty to seek God for our true calling and walk in it so that our gift can truly make room for us.

Chapter 6

HIDDEN TREASURE

Greatly Valued & Highly Prized

Before I conclude the first half of this book, I want to share a revelation I took from proverbs 18:22 that really inspired me to become an advocate for women. The New Living Translation of this verse gave me a different view of how I should see a woman. It says, "The man who finds a wife finds a treasure and receives favor from the Lord." The original transliterated word for wife means woman, female, or opposite of man.[21] Wow! This proverb implies that not only is a wife a treasure, but every individual female is a treasure waiting to be found! A treasure in this context is someone who is greatly valued and highly prized! My voice tone has gone up several decibels now because that is not how the average man sees a female, especially if he is heavily influenced by the culture of the game.

On August 30th, 2010, "My Mic Sounds Nice: A Truth about Women and Hip Hop" premiered on BET which chronicled the history of female MCs from the early eighties through about two-thousand ten. As I watched the documentary, I remembered my childhood in the eighties where MC Lyte, Roxanne Shonté, and Queen Latifah were among the few female rap artists who were big on the scene. Past and present, female rappers have competed in a male dominated industry where women are required to have something special and unique just to be considered good as their male counterparts. The raw talent of a woman has been de-emphasized as not enough for mass media appeal. Desperation mixed with the increasingly low self-image of society has made it easier to promote visual glamour and *sexism*, with regard to female entertainers. Very few women have succeeded without becoming a victim of *sexism*, and others were simply not willing to allow the culture of the game to permeate their souls, so they withdrew. And yet, others saw moral virtue as the opportunity cost or tradeoff that must be paid in order to obtain a certain level of success in the industry.

Women have been exploited for selfish profits to the

point where it is almost expected. Most women today are aware of the fact that sex sells, and very few thrive in the entertainment industry without becoming a sexual product. Of course *sexism* is prevalent in other industries, but entertainment seems to be leading the pack. One female rap artist interviewed on the documentary really highlighted this potential tradeoff when she commented on the idea that the industry and its customers do not want to see women in baggy jeans; it wants to see women sexy. She also expressed feelings that her male counterparts do not see the female as someone to learn from, but rather someone to look at.[22] I would add that the glamour and *sexism* monster has always been lurking around the corners of each generation, promoting the culture of the game. And as time moved forward, the true treasure of a woman has been pounced upon, by the overwhelming fascination with modified beauty and held back by the claws of sexual discrimination.

Regardless of the industry, women have always helped men succeed, and all we have to do to prove it is look at the success of any prominent male figure. Women will always be the embodiment of beauty and glamour, but, more importantly let us not forget that they are the lifeblood of our success as men. The great value and prize of a woman has a lot to do with the fact that without her, we as men could not fulfill our vision in life. There is no way we can live and succeed without the help of a woman. She is our passageway into life itself, and that alone makes her a treasure.

Treasure Hunters

Oftentimes when a man finds a woman, like a buried treasure, she may not shine, sparkle, and glisten to her full potential. Many women feel buried by the pressures of this culture, but the sentiment that I sense from listening to women is that they are not proud of the choices this culture pressures most to make. These life choices have acted like camouflage, which makes it difficult to see the treasure that innately resides in a woman. Camouflage is intended to deceive an enemy by altering or obscuring the appearance so that it blends in with the background. So it has become in this culture, as the pain of two-story stilettos is placed above the comfort of being casual. Since we know that the culture of the game is our enemy, its expectations should be much clearer. Women must breast feed through implants, sleep in make-up, and wake up in wigs just to satisfy this enemy.

A man who thinks like a treasure hunter knows that every woman is a treasure no matter how deep the culture of the game has tried to bury her. He knows that a woman is not a video vixen, prostitute, stripper, porn star, or whatever else this culture designates her to be. He knows that when he finds a treasure he must polish it, because it is worth something. As a matter of fact, when a man sees a woman as the treasure that she really is, he will see her as rare and priceless because there is no other woman exactly like her anywhere.

When I first met my wife, I did not realize the treasure that I had found. The key understanding is that even though I did not see her as a treasure, the fact remained that she was a treasure. When she was born and being held in her mother's arms, she was a treasure then waiting to be found. When she was being chased by little boys during recess in elementary school, she was a treasure then waiting to be found. When her father would take her to the annual Veiled Prophet Fourth of July Fair on the St. Louis riverfront, she was a treasure then. Every female in your City, State and world is a treasure, and should be treated as such. The culture of the game has distorted the virtuousness of a woman by exploiting her body, minimizing her mind, and grieving her spirit. Instead of finding a treasure, we are burying a treasure even deeper every time we disregard a woman's value.

I am challenging every man who reads this book not to tear the woman down, but to lift her up and make her shine, and I guarantee she will make you shine even brighter. No matter what society projects, a woman is not a whore, tramp, trick, or a piece of meat. Every woman is not your treasure, but every woman is a treasure. If you are not going to treat her as a treasure, leave her for the man who will. The truth is she will forever be a treasure no matter the choices she has made or what she has been through.

What Women Want

If life was an elevator, the truth would bring you up and a lie would bring you down. You should at least agree by now that relationship games could not exist apart from lying. When two people value the truth, they can have a successful relationship and go up together. When you apply the truth of God's word to your relationship, you are making a spiritual connection that sets you apart from the evil nature of a lie. So ladies, start by being truthful with your self. Apart from physical attraction, ask your self what really draws you to a man? I will go out on a limb and say that you do not want a man who is sorry, lazy, womanizing, or abusive. Have you ever admired a man for being totally dependent on a woman for his lifelong survival? I think not, but that is exactly what the culture of the game has taught many men. Some men are so consumed with the fantasies this culture projects that they have lost touch with reality. A real man lives in the reality that successful relationships take work, and he is willing to put in that work. I will go out even further on the same limb and say that as a woman you want a man who is driven. The question then becomes "what is he driven by?"

I believe every woman really wants a man that is driven, but more importantly, every woman wants one that is driven by God. Before you deny this fact, think about it. Regardless of what a woman believes, the essential characteristics that she is drawn to would be the quintessential traits of the Spirit of God. Love, joy, peace, longsuffering, gentleness, goodness, faith, meekness and self-control are all part of the nature of God.[23] Whether a woman believes in God or not, how can she deny a man with those qualities? So, before you even think about getting into a relationship, if you want to have a better chance at success, find out if the person values the truth. This is your best defense against the culture of the game. I say this because as single ladies, the more you are set apart by the truth, the faster you can receive a real man who is driven by the true nature of God. To be driven by God is different from being religious. To say you believe in God is totally different from being driven by God. To be driven is to be moved by force. In this case, the truth of God's word is the force that moves you. The more you know the truth, the more you strive to live in the truth wholeheartedly and with determination. Anyone can acquire this drive by giving his or her attention to the principles of God's word and allowing it to set him or her apart from the evil nature that is inherent in lies. As single men, the more you are set apart by the truth, the more you will see women as the treasures they are. Truth is the only protection we have against the culture of the game.

I have stated that 72 percent of American between the ages of 18 and 25 believe there is no absolute truth. Maybe you consider yourself to be driven, just not by God. Well, "what drives you?" is your question to answer. But I am attempting to persuade you, or simply confirm in your thinking, that every woman wants a real man who is not just religious, but driven by God. I repeat, even if you do not believe in God, the qualities women want in a man are the ones that are representative of a man who is driven by God. Let me give you one specific example of a quality that women want in men so badly that they will overlook everything else because of it.

For just a moment, picture any male superstar who is extremely unattractive, foul-mouthed, and has a personality that would normally act as a female repellent in the average everyday "unheard-of guy" circle. Ok, do you have that male in mind? Now, let's answer the question, why does that unsightly, foul-mouthed, male superstar attract so many women who want to marry him and have his baby? The answer is "vision," although you were probably thinking money. Money is only a byproduct of vision. But I believe every woman is fundamentally attracted to vision.[24] Since that guy you have in mind has probably at some point rightfully thanked God at an awards show, they have to believe as I do, that God gives us all the talent we need to pursue His vision for our lives.

The crossroads and forks of life exist because of the fact that God has given us all free will; therefore, people can rebel against God and choose to use their gifts and talents for something other than what God intended. Remember, if God had not given us the freedom to exercise our will, everyone would be morally good and there would be no *sovereignty*, no freedom, and no supreme excellence in a God that we had no choice but to serve. Consequently, thousands of people are being entertained by someone with an altered vision that has been influenced by a very low level of thinking. Nonetheless, people are still attracted to vision, especially if the vision leads to riches. The next time you ask what seems to be a baffling question, remind yourself that when a man has talent and vision, he does not have to be attractive to attract an array of women. Just because a man chooses a path that leads to fame and fortune, it does not mean that it was the right path to take, especially when you take in account what was done to get there.

The New Living Bible Translation of Jeremiah 29:11 reads, "For I know the plans I have for you, says the Lord. They are plans for good and not for disaster, to give you a future and a hope." Even though you do not know the fullness of what God's plan is for your life, He did say that He has a plan for your life. His plan is not only the future you hope for, but it is good! It is good for you and good for others. The question is do you really trust God with your future? Those of us who trust Him are also driven by Him in our thoughts and our actions. Nothing is off limits. His ways become ours ways. His words become our words; and what pleases Him becomes what pleases us. When your gifts and talents are aligned with God, how much more will you be free from the guilty past that may have gotten you to that wealth or the insatiable motive of lust that can only be sustained by chasing more riches? The blessing of God, however, makes a person rich, and he adds no sorrow with it. [25]

You may not be able to control the culture in this big world, but you can control what you allow in your little world; so stand firm on principle and not preference. Ephesians 6:14 starts by saying, "Stand therefore, having your loins girded about with truth." Can you see that truth is first and foremost? The culture of the game is all around you; it is your enemy and you have to stand against its lies with truth. The loin is the part of the body that is regarded as the seat of physical strength, procreative and *regenerative* power.[21] To gird one's loins with truth is to be ready to combat any lie that threatens the purity of your moral, spiritual, and physical existence, as well as that of the human race. Metaphorically, every offensive and defensive weapon is hinged on the belt of truth. If each woman reading this book would embrace the truth that you are a treasure, your individual stand will be a stand well worth taking to project truth back into the self-image of society and protect your virtue from the culture of the game.

What Men Want

Real men seem to be hidden as well. Some women may even say that a real man does not exist, but they would be wrong. Both men and women alike are pressured by the culture of the game, but men tend to have a greater propensity to become driven by it. I believe it is because men have an inborn desire to conquer any challenge we face in this world. It is in our nature to show off the victory of a successful hunt. I recommend reading an outstanding book called *Love and Respect: The Love She Most Desires, the Respect He Desperately Needs* by Dr. Emerson Eggerichs. It explains how we fulfill our need for respect. Men feel respected when we are acknowledged for something positive that we have done. Acknowledgment is the key to communicating respect to a man. We want and need to hear statements of gratitude and admiration which in turn encourages us to conquer even more.

I played on several sports teams from middle school through my college years and it was very important that my peers respected me as a team member. The greater the feeling of respect as an athlete the better I performed on that team. Respect or the lack thereof, translates strongly to a man's feeling of worth and can be the reason for success or failure in his relationships. The most humiliating thing a woman can do is disregard a man's worth. It is so important for some men to feel respected that they would rather die fighting for it than live without it. A gang member for instance, may be seen as morally degenerate, but young men who join gangs are willing to face early death because they feel life is not worth living if respect is irredeemably lost. No matter how inappropriate the expression that secures respect, whether selling wolf tickets or shooting someone dead, a strong need for respect continues to encourage their self-harming decision to gang bang.

The culture of the game also suggests a way of living that encourages young boys all over the world to turn to *womanizing* as a way of fulfilling this need for respect. More and more young boys are being lured into the game under the deception that over the top sexuality such as "hit it and quit it," fast money, and material possessions are emblematic of manhood. These boys eventually become men but never grow to the realization of what being a real man is all about.

My advice to men is to view women in the light of what I call my normal five: mother, sister, wife, daughter or female friend. That covers every type of woman a man would ever encounter. These are the women that the average descent guy would not want to hurt. If a guy does not care about his own mother, that is not normal! I've seen and read about some of the most notorious men who abused women, but would die for their own mother or daughter. Even Adolf Hitler, whose ideal view of women was treacherous, had reverence for his own mother.

Giving a man what he needs may not seem noteworthy when two people are dating because the binding covenant we talked about earlier is not there. For those of us who make a marriage commitment, we look for our wives to reassure our worth almost constantly. This is why finances are the number one thing couples fight about. Unfortunately, finances have become the quintessential measure of a man's worth. When men feel worthless, it usually manifests itself in silence, which results in a loss of communication. As you may know, a relationship can not work without open lines of communication, but men have a hard time communicating openly with women who project a sense of worthlessness towards them. Men need to hear that they are worth something, and sometimes we need to hear it without having to ask. Feelings of worthlessness can cause any relationship to take a turn for the worse.

Ladies, here is a little secret that is not to be used selfishly, but with all sincerity. When words of respect, admiration, and worth are spoken to a man, he will want to spend his life with you because those words encourage the champion in him. Such words sincerely spoken can open a man's eyes to view a woman as a potential wife. You can be the most beautiful woman in the world, but if your man feels regarded by you as worthless, he will never view you as a wife. Although I enjoy wealth as much as the next person, worth is more powerful than wealth. Wealth is how valuable I am relative to this world's financial system. Worth, however, is how valuable I am to people. So, if a woman is doing a fantastic job at making her man feel valued and he still does not want to spend the rest of his life with her, consider one of two things: Either he is playing games on purpose or you have violated something on his infamous list that he just can not settle down with.

If you take this book seriously, you will begin to know what a real man is all about. And I hope you can see that it is not about being a player. I mentioned earlier that all men are not dogs. I want to also add some balance to that statement as you approach the second half of this book. It may sound like I'm advocating perfection, but I am not. I know as well as you that no man is perfect. We guys do not have it all together; we will make mistakes, we will miss the mark from time to time, but remember, the key point I make throughout this book will continue to be that truth is the protective barrier that sets you apart from the culture of the game. If two people value the truth, the relationship can work, even in the midst of your imperfections.

Beneath The Surface

I gleaned the phrase, "sediment of grace" from a novice understanding of the modern archaeological study of sedimentary processes. Sediment is a naturally-occurring material deposit that is the source of sedimentary rocks. The sediment accumulating on rocks can preserve the remains of past life. Archeologists refer to these remains as fossil records. Past experiences are like sediment, preserving both the good and the bad from a relationship. Between the numerous storms of life, the unfortunate actions of people, and the overall influence of the culture of the game; many of us have yet to discover the true treasure that exists in others. However, there is hope as these sort of sedimentary layers of life can be chiseled away, revealing what has been hidden for so long.

Some layers get formed by the hottest seasonal fashion that can redefine a person's self-image without the person ever having a say about his or her own style. Although everyone does not fit the current fashion trends, many people are losing themselves by jumping on the band wagon, regardless of their personal preference or body type. Maybe layers are formed when we endeavor to build reputations for ourselves that are not consistent with our true character. And more than likely, layers get formed as the multiple masks that we wear cover the authentic beauty of our true personalities.

Similar to modern archaeology, the cost of recovery, preservation and conservation of some relationships can be enormous. Whether you admit it or not, most people approach a new relationship like an archaeologist, seeking to find out more about the other person. Some of us have relationship remains scattered across a large territory. We have been damaged by several "relation-shipwrecks," but little rebuilding has taken place in our lives between then and now. We know that wreckage can not recover itself, but as the average person navigates through the raging waves of a progressive relationship, we realize that none of us are very well-equipped to venture into the deep sea of someone else's past. Simply put, when two people who have experienced any number of tumultuous "relation-shipwrecks," only the grace of God can recover the treasure that has sunk within.

Restoring the treasure within us while actively involved in a relationship requires that two people get to know one another without the interference of their personal fulfillment objectives. The best way I have found to accomplish that is to approach relationships in phasing. As you move from one phase to the next in the relationship process, you will notice those aforementioned layers of sediment start to chip away. Some people will have more layers than others, but we all have things in our past that may surface as the relationship progresses. As we wrap up the first part of this book, we must understand that both men and women alike carry around some degree of hurt from past experiences which tend to follow them from one relationship to the next.

Regardless of how these experiences are fossilized, if we do not deal with past hurts they will become layered with fear. As we begin fishing for new love, these fears will eventually show up on the surface of our next relationship, and each person involved will be just as shocked as when bad things happen to good people. As past fears continue to surface, they add a degree of doubt and pose a threat to what could be a potentially good relationship. No one goes into a relationship eager to share all the negative experiences of his or her past. Consequently, we have learned to suppress those fears while neglectfully waiting for others to trigger the irrational behavior lying dormant within us. Some people have experienced relationship catastrophes of titanic proportions, while others have slowly accumulated several minor shipwrecks of unresolved issues over a period of years. Either way, our past fears become a warning that something similar could happen in our future relationships; therefore, we dress ourselves up before jumping back into the next relationship, careful not to expose our bloody wounds to the sharks.

As we enjoy ourselves in the sea of love, we do so dressed in the best "relationship wet suit" we can find. The problem is that our tailored Armani suits, Abercrombie tees, designer jeans, and all the top spring fashion accessories provide little protection as we meet face to face with the deepest, wettest, internal fears of our past. These are the shark bites that we are still waiting to heal. The way we dress as surface dwellers does not provide buoyancy or thermal insulation when a relationship sinks coldly below sea level. It does not protect us from the abrasive words of the painful finish. And the masks that we wear can take many forms, but provide little oxygen in the profound depths of a relationship. We continue to come up for air, trying to exhale from under the pressure of past experiences that have shaped our current thinking, only to remind ourselves of the risk we are taking and how wounded we really are. Other examples of the internal sharks that prevent us from going deeper in relationships, which many of us are struggling with today, are as follows:

"I'll never be good enough for him."
"He's probably playing games just like the last guy."
"She just wants me for my fame and money."
"Why would he want me when I have kids?"

These and other issues keep us on the surface, which allows us to avoid the underlined fear of being rejected. We are so ill-equipped that we do not want to go deeper in a relationship. The intimate, emotional, and sexual expressions that were once reserved for true love have now evolved into the surface encounters and fantasy fishing we see in relationships today. Instead of deep intimate commitment with one's life mate, we have settled for dating as a sport; and when we are done with the fish, we simply take it off the hook and cast it back into the sea of love despite how bruised it may be. No wonder the average person has a fear of commitment, to say the least.

Maybe you have been told to deal with these internal issues before you get into a serious relationship, and I agree to a certain extent. Fortunately, there is help available for people struggling with addictions, low self-esteem, childhood trauma, fear of commitment, and the like. But remember, even if you get help for obvious surface issues, relationships have a way of bringing up deep internal issues that you did not even know about yourself! With that understanding, at some point there will be fears, doubts, and emotions that have to be confronted while active in a relationship. Unfortunately, the freedom and safety to confront these issues are induced by marriage, which is another reason why half of all marriages fail. In a marriage relationship, couples can become extremely overwhelmed by how challenging it is to overcome their combined issues. This is why valuing the truth is the most import ingredient for success, and taking relationships in phases can create that free and safe environment, giving a potential marriage a fighting chance.

I have learned that denouncing the game really starts with valuing the truth. Therefore, when my wife asks me a question I am able to give her what she is asking for, the truth. Because I understand how much she can help, no longer am I afraid that she will add to my challenging day.

Instead, she makes my day better. When I'm done talking with her, I feel like I can conquer the world. Like a modern day Rocky Balboa looking to his corner, I am always inspired by my wife to conquer life's challenges.

Understand that wanting to be truthful in your relationship is not enough to stop the game, we have to do something. Remember to denounce, discern and dodge the game every time it comes your way. If you have not taken the time to give the bible a serious read, I encourage you to start with the book of proverbs. The wisdom enclosed in those thirty-one chapters helped change the way I view women. Most importantly, it changed the way I view my wife, daughter, mother, sister and female friends. As it suggests, women are indeed the most valuable treasure a man could ever find.

Bite Size

- Women will always be the embodiment of beauty and glamour, but more importantly let's not forget that they are the lifeblood of our success as men.
- There is no way we can live and succeed without the help of a woman. She is our passageway into life itself, and that alone makes her a treasure.
- The culture of the game has distorted the virtuousness of a woman by exploiting her body and minimizing her mind and spirit.
- Every woman is not your treasure. But every woman is a treasure, no matter the choices she has made or what she has been through.
- Truth is the only protection you have against the culture of the game.
- As single men, the more you are set apart by the truth, the more you will see women as the treasures they are.
- As single ladies, the more you are set apart by the truth, the faster you can receive a real man that is driven by true Godly qualities.

- Anyone can acquire this drive by giving his or her attention to the principles of God's word and allowing it to set them apart from the evil nature that is inherent in lies.
- If each woman reading this book would embrace the revelation that you are a treasure, your individual stand will be a stand well worth taking to project truth back into the self-image of society and protect your virtue from the culture of the game.

Part  Two

PHASING OUT THE GAME

The A.F.I.E.M **Approach**

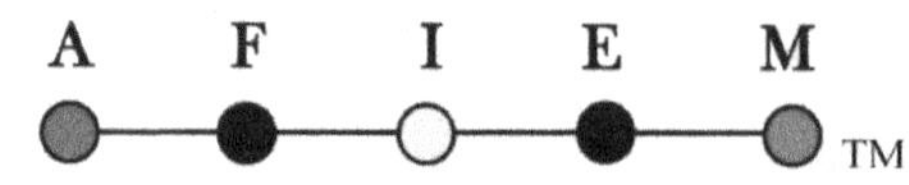

A new approach to successful relationships.

Chapter 7

THE AFIEM APPROACH

Red, Yellow, Green

In the second half of this book I will attempt to take you on a visual journey. Let's start by referring to the color version of the AFIEM diagram on the back cover of this book. You will notice that there are five points which represent the five phases of a relationship: acquaintance, friendship, intimacy, engagement and marriage. There is a solid line that flows through each point representing the un-ending need for communication at each phase of the AFIEM approach. Each point contains its own set of boundaries that I will define as we focus on each individual phase. The colors red, yellow, and green represent the different degrees of behavior, boundaries and communication as you progress from one phase of a relationship to the next. I associated the universal stop light color of red with the acquaintance phase, so as to place this phase under the most intense restrictions. The **acquaintance** phase involves slight knowledge of a person, maybe a first encounter or periodic encounters with a person you have come to know by personal contact or through a response to something that is clearly casual. The red stop light should be figuratively illuminated at this point with regard to dating, courting, going steady, or whatever you call an exclusive relationship. As the acquaintance phase is given adequate soak time, it could progress into the beginning stages of a friendship, but the degree of restriction should still fall within the red stop zone.

Friendship should be regarded as the most important phase of a relationship, but the average couple takes it too lightly or skips over this phase altogether while becoming exclusive at a time when friendship should be the primary focus. Therefore, I have also placed the friendship phase near the stop zone to restrict the establishment of an exclusive relationship. Just because a couple enters into an exclusive dating relationship, it doesn't mean they have a friendship. Most of us know from experience that when an exclusive dating relationship is over, usually the friendship is also over. However, each phase after friendship should progress on a sliding scale, with relatively less restrictions as more trust is earned, which will preserve the relationship. The yellow caution zone has been reserved for the **intimacy** and **engagement** phases, while the color green is reserved for the **marriage** phase. Below are three good reasons why approaching relationships in phases work.

1. **Phases act like a return policy for relationships:** When you meet someone for the first time you really do not know what to expect. Phases allow you the opportunity to see in real time whether a person can keep a commitment and give you the chance to live with a particular commitment without living with the person. If that person can not commit to the terms of a successful FRIENDSHIP, he or she can always be returned to being a lifetime acquaintance.
2. **Phases work like a second opinion for relationships:** No need to ask your girlfriend what she thinks about him, because after all, she's not the one spending time with him. As you devote adequate time to each phase, your decision to move forward in a relationship will be clearly defined. We all have one opinion of a person as an

acquaintance and a different opinion of that person as a friend or mate. Each phase that you give adequate soak time to will provide a perspective from a different angle and therefore render a second, third, and even a fourth opinion. Each phase will bring you closer to knowing who he really is, regardless of that illusive first impression.

3. **Phases help avoid relationship games:** Do not take it personally if a player is not willing to continue these phases of a successful relationship. It is actually a good thing because it allows you to cut your losses early and move on to the man or woman who is not playing any games. A player is not looking for a successful relationship and therefore will not have time or patience for these phases. This is exactly what you want because you do not have time for playing games.

Since the source of the game is lying, allow adequate time for each phase of AFIEM and never skip from one phase to the next. This raises the age old question, "how long should one date before marriage?" Well, if you really take these phases seriously, it has to be relative to the amount of time one has to devote to another. The continuous line of communication along with the establishment of the appropriate boundaries within each phase forces us to focus on behavior, recognize behavior, and control behavior as the relationship progresses. It is much easier on the soul to approach relationships in phases that have predefined boundaries. The AFIEM approach contains all of these elements and more, providing a better chance of success by phasing out the game altogether. It protects the mental, emotional, and spiritual well-being of those involved. In each phase of AFIEM one must be true to oneself as well as others in answering the question, "where do I want to go from here?" When two people who value the truth agree to follow this approach, positive adjustments will be made concerning the future state and timing in which their relationship progresses. If they choose to phase out the game, there is no reason to meet today and marry tomorrow, because phases take time. This truth is what preserves the treasure in you and provides freedom for your soul. I pray that you are ready to denounce the game and reveal the treasure that exists within.

Boundaries

When we fail to set boundaries, we open the door to the culture of the game. Imagine for just a moment that your quest for a successful relationship has brought you before two large doors. The door on the left leads to your quintessential soul-mate relationship and the door on the right lead to total devastation. Everything you know about relationships, whether good or bad is about to weigh in on your decision. There is no turning back as you study the two doors carefully. You notice the door on the left has the letter "A" meticulously centered on the door and engraved in 24 karat gold. However, you have no idea that this door leads to your soul mate. Therefore, you take a careful look at the door to your right. This door is somewhat wider and has a few more visual details than the other. A sparkling diamond coated letter "I" is attached slightly above center. There is a small window framed in various jewels just above the letter "I," tempting you to take a peek through. As you lean into the glass with your hands cradled along side your eyes, you see several attractive people. In an attempt to sharpen your view, you press into the glass causing the door to crack open ever so slightly, revealing the soft and soothing sound of music playing in the background.

You realize that this door was not locked and wonder if that is the case for the door to your left. So you decide to step back and reassess your choices. You move again to the left and stretch forth your hand to check door "A" for access only to discover that it is locked. It makes you wonder, "is there something special lurking behind door 'A'?" Why is it locked whereas door "I" is open? As you continue to examine door "A", you find that you overlooked a small intercom with a button that says, "Press to talk." Not sure what you will say, you turn again to the door on the right. So much is happening behind door "I," and it sounds like everyone is having a "feel good" time inside. You cautiously push door "I" open to further enhance your view. The allure of the sensual sound increases. There are glamorously dressed people waving you into the dim lit room that is intimately arranged in the most seductive setting. You take one final glimpse at door "A" but you are so persuaded by the soft and soothing, easy feel good moment behind door "I" that you enter, charmed and ready to indulge, as it gently closes behind you.

This imaginary story may seem a little exaggerated, but it is not that far from what happens in relationships today. Door "A" represents the acquaintance phase, and how the progression from acquaintance to friendship requires more talking than touching. The push to talk intercom on door "A" illustrates how your personal locks and boundaries should always be in place at the start of any relationship; and that communication is the key that opens the door to each relationship phase. Many have become impatient with the idea of opening one door at a time, especially when established locks and boundaries are in the way of their personal fulfillment objective. Remember, respecting boundaries, observing behavior and communication is part of the work of a successful relationship. When a player is looking for the shortest route to his or her personal fulfillment objective, an open door is always inviting. Know that there is nothing wrong with you if your relationship doors are not open to just anything. An acquaintance door should naturally progress into a friendship, and each phase should hold the key to the next door.

On the other hand, door "I" represents intimacy and how quickly people are seduced into this door with little knowledge of what's on the inside. Very little communication took place before the decision was made to enter into the door of intimacy. If most people entering into the intimacy phase are strangers, the people they become intimate with are nothing more than acquaintances anyway. You may have noticed that I did not mention a door "F" for friendship at all because friendship is relatively disregarded. The truth is that friendship is exactly where the foundation for a successful relationship is established. Friendship should come after making someone's acquaintance, but this most important phase is skipped over like the marked square in a hopscotch game and that square is marked with the key to the door of intimacy.

We all know that the average dating relationship is not based on friendship; instead, it swings on the hinges of intimacy, which is why there are so many people in and out of this door who never knew each other to begin with. Over the years I've observed intimacy to be the most anticipated, the most abused and, unfortunately the most misunderstood phase of the relationship process. We must understand that boundaries not only serve to protect, but will also become your virtual lab for testing whether or not you can trust one another in a more intimate relationship. It may seem that setting boundaries will cause a person to lie or play games, but really, it is just the opposite. Boundaries are a part of our defense system against the culture of the game, and when we fail to set boundaries we leave the doors of our relationship open to the evil nature of lies.

Juxtaposed, when we set boundaries we force ourselves and the people we are involved with to live in the truth. You may be thinking, "How is that so? If there are no boundaries then people would not have to lie to get around them, right?" Wrong. You have to actually set boundaries and experience the benefit of this tactic for yourself in order to fully understand this point. It is like viewing a landscape from a higher point on a mountain as opposed to the valley. Boundaries allow us to see our relationships from a much better perspective. Without boundaries we have no set of conditions in which we commit to entrust another.

When boundaries are enforced they afford us a way to measure trust within ourselves and others. As a matter of fact, boundaries help establish the same environment in our relationships that was created for Adam and Eve. Remember, God used the words "where are you?" to question Adam's spiritual position of leadership and authority. In a natural relationship, obligation and responsibility must also be questioned in order to ensure our position of trust. Therefore, boundaries appeal to both the spiritual and the practical side of the question, "Where are you?" When boundaries are set in your relationship, a person's sense of obligation and responsibility towards you can be measured, and the proof of their words will help move the relationship forward.

This leads to the contrasting thought that broken boundaries afford us a way to measure the trustworthiness within ourselves and others. Words can activate a sense of trust that may be based on deception, but actions support the sincerity of those words as they are tested. Therefore, the more boundaries that are broken, the less worthy one becomes of trust. If a person uses lies disguised as the truth, do not worry, because clear boundaries will help test the truth. And just as any other test, if one does not pass, he or she should not be given the key to the next door. We should view respect of boundaries as the test of trustworthiness that must be passed in order to progress to the next phase of the relationship. Here are a few qualities that boundaries can test:

- **Boundaries allow you to test the patience of yourself and others.** Double lines on a two-way street represent a "no passing zone" but drivers who are impatient or in a hurry may ignore those boundaries in hopes that a careful pass will ensure that no one will get hurt. When established boundaries are broken at any phase of a relationship we put ourselves and others in danger of getting hurt. Even if nothing harmful happens when certain boundaries are broken, know that your carefulness has little to do with your protection. Breaking one boundary only makes it easier to break the next, and before long your protection against the game will become as effective as someone walking through a slightly opened door.

- **Boundaries allow you to test the integrity of yourself and others.** Observing whether or not one stays within boundaries enhances your ability to discern their personal integrity. Since trust has to be earned, what better way to assess integrity than examining how one adheres to established boundaries? The acquaintance phase is the best time to enforce your strictest boundaries. If an acquaintance questions your boundaries, feel free to tell him or her it is not open for discussion. You are not obligated to explain your boundaries to an acquaintance. People who do not respect your boundaries should be lifetime acquaintances anyway. Why move to the next phase of friendship with people who are boundary breakers? Boundary breakers ultimately become covenant breakers.[26]
- **Boundaries allow you to test the relational intelligence of a person.** When a driver comes to an intersection where there is a blinking red light at a four-way stop instead of a traditional set of traffic lights, he should approach the intersection as if it was a four-way stop sign, come to a complete stop,

yield to traffic that was there before, and cross when the intersection is clear. Those who wait for the blinking red light to turn green must be ignorant of this general rule. LOL! Ok, on a more serious note. I have found myself questioning the intelligence of drivers who come to such a stop and speed through the intersection, disregarding the next car in the observed progression. For me, this is standard driving etiquette, so when this rule is not respected, I contribute it to poor driver's education or blatant disregard. In the same way, there are certain boundaries and general rules that we expect people to observe in relationships. Let's face it; we all have certain standards that must be met in order to consider being in a relationship with someone, and if a person does not meet our standards, he or she is simply not considered for a serious relationship.

Behavior

People behave in various ways depending on the circumstances and respond according to their internal or external influences. This makes it very important that we focus on behavior at each phase of a relationship and never take words at face value until they are tested, especially the statement "I love you." Even God looks at behavior when it comes to those three words. He says, "If you love me, keep my commandments,"[27] and that "our love for one another will prove to the world that we are his disciples."[28] That sounds like the ultimate litmus test, because "I love you" is only a statement until we observe the behavior associated with those words. Ladies, from God's perspective, man is commanded to love the woman. This means you have the right to be loved. You deserve to be loved. You were made to be loved. Therefore, you should be just as excited about seeing love in action as you are about hearing the words "I love you."

We have the power to put love in action with the five phases of the AFIEM approach, because there is no one who will take the time to go through each of these phases if he or she is not serious about you, does not mean you any good, and does not love you. Basically, any player who is selfishly seeking to fulfill his or her own personal objective would not subscribe to the AFIEM approach because it is not the shortest route from point A to their destination. Also, people who play games are not trying to take things one phase at a time, and such a scenic approach would be a colossal waste of their time.

In traditional dating relationships we can become so nonchalant about how people act that we accept behavior that should be unacceptable. For instance, people say things that they do not really mean and make promises they do not plan to keep. How often do we plan to get together with others but never follow through? Not following through is a behavior you can observe. Often we are afraid to confront people for breaking promises or for never following through and simply register those people in our mind as someone not to take seriously. People say to me quite often "let's get together and do lunch," and quite often I respond with, "ok, let's do that; give me a call and we'll set a date." Do we really want to have lunch? Or, has that just become the common and acceptable way to respond? Whether or not the person calls, confirms a lunch date, and shows up is observable behavior.

I have coined the phrase among my circle that "people do what they want to do, when they want to do it, as long as there is nothing stopping them." Think about it; even if a person is not initially motivated, with the right set of internal or external influences he or she will find a way to respond. For instance, if a person does not respond to my invitation for lunch, there is only one of three things that I can do. I can conclude that I am not a strong enough external influence and stop trying, find a way to provide the incentive that will solicit the response that I desire, or conclude that something is really stopping the person from responding. Conversely, if I was not serious about getting together with a person, I probably would not make any extra effort to follow-up with the person either. This nonchalant way of relating seems to have become the norm in society, but it doesn't have to make it into our relationships as long as we are truthful with ourselves and others.

SALT

Behavior and boundaries are two of three common threads that exist in each phase of the AFIEM approach. Boundaries work like a virtual lab which allows behavior to be tested in different situations and circumstances. Whether negative or positive, good or bad, we all see people in terms of behavior. For instance, one might ask of Fred, "what type of person is Wilma?" That question is obviously relative, but never the less, the answer is based on behavior. I believe we all have a mental database that automatically records the behavior of others. The problem is that every person's behavior will change in respect to their environment. Our behavior can change from one extreme to another depending on the perceived boundaries; hence the reason people act differently in church than they do in a night club. At each phase of the AFIEM approach, it is up to you to establish and maintain the appropriate boundaries within the relationship, making it possible to observe and test behavior under different circumstances. The best way to accomplish this is by incorporating the third common thread called "communication." Communication is used to compare what is said to what is actually done.

Although behavior is very important, you must be wise in how you conduct yourself around people who do not think or believe as you do in order to make good use of your time. It is possible to be viewed as the hard-nosed, aggravating, religious hypocrite that no one wants to be around. Consequently, our talk must be with grace, mixed with salt, so that we may be able to have conversation with anyone.[29] In other words, we must behave wisely and bridle our tongues with words of grace, carefully using those words as if they are the seasoning for our overall conversations.

Salt and communication may be a world apart in practical usage, but they are parallel in several senses. Just as salt is to food, communication is to a relationship. In recognition that salt makes food taste better; communication makes a relationship better. In the sense that salt preserves food; communication preserves a relationship. Salt can be used as a bonding agent; communication can be used to bond with people. Salt makes people thirsty; communication mixed with grace and seasoned with salt makes one thirst for more of a person.

This wisdom should be applied in all of our conversations, because how we communicate with people can open the door for hurt or healing. Words can inspire the purity of who we are as individuals, helping us to develop into our authentic selves; or they can reinforce the culture of the game, promoting a deceptive imitation of personal identity. Words can be a powerful concentration of nourishment or a destructive poison. Therefore, we need wisdom and grace to know how to refine our words for human consumption. There is no better use of our time than speaking words that empower instead of devour, preserve instead of spoil, bond instead of separate, create savor as opposed to bitterness, and thirst in place of indifference. Communication is the salt of any relationship.

In the first half of this book I talked about the culture of the game and how it reinforces the self-image of society, regardless of how irrational it may be. We scratched the surface of the ever changing external influences of mass media and how society reacts to it. I would like for you to view the first half of this book as if it is the game tape of your opponent and I am the quintessential coach that wants nothing less than to lead you to victory. Successful coaches review tapes to study the patterns of aggressive and defensive behavior of their opponent in order to develop a success plan. In relationships, the culture of the game is your opponent, and it is just as important to know that culture as it is to know yourself. When you denounce the game, you position yourself to discern the game, and when you discern the game, you position yourself to dodge the game. The AFIEM approach seeks success by avoiding the game altogether, but you must understand that it is still your responsibility to execute the plan both offensively and defensively in order to avoid the so called *pimps*, *players*, *macks*, *big ballers* and *shot callers* that will inevitably come your way.

The Lover's Shopping List

For the remainder of this journey we will compare relationships to shopping. Have you ever been told that you are not flexible enough with your list of relationship requirements? What is the one thing on your list that you just can not compromise? Ok, now what is the other thing?

I'm sure you have at least one more thing right? My point is that some of us really do have the infamous list! For instance, he has to be a certain height or she has to have a certain body type to say the least. Even the top IQ score can be a factor for some; nothing is too far fetched to leave off the list. One guy I interviewed told me that he cheated on his wife. I ask why and his answer was that he had married below his intelligence level. I found out through further conversation that he cheated with a waitress, not to say that a waitress is not intelligent, but I'm sure he did not have sex with her because she whipped out a high IQ score and flew him to the moon for a sexual fantasy that was out of this world. We can go on and on about the array of attributes that make up someone's perfect lover's list, but what I've found is that our list would be of greater value if we saw it as a list of things that makes us vulnerable.

People who are dead set on a list of attributes are much more vulnerable to the game, because their attention becomes directed only to those who fit their list. Of all the wonderful people that could be a potential life-mate, relationship shoppers typically focus on people who market their assets the best and overlook people whose assets are not so obvious. The initial perception of people who do not reflect our list of attributes is commonly referred to as "not my type," but no matter how well or badly someone is packaged, quite frankly our type is determined by the testing of boundaries, observation of behaviors and continuous communication, period. This is why our shopping list should be seen as a list of our own vulnerabilities that could propel us into a vulnerable situation. When we view our list of attributes as must haves, it narrows our focus and eliminates a group of exceptional human beings from which we could have met our soul mate. Now to be honest with ourselves, many of us have longed for someone who seemed to be the embodiment of our list only to find out later that they were conceited, stuck up, careless, stupid, crazy and even married already.

According to soulmates.com, "Research shows that in less than 30 seconds of our first encounter we tend to form a preliminary impression of people. The first impression is based 55 percent on appearance, 7 percent on words we use during the course of our conversation, and 38 percent on the tone of the voice. This configuration shows that even before we get sufficient time to demonstrate our abilities, the first impression is already cast within a few seconds, and the main considerations for this first impression are clothes, body language and attitude." People can be very self-conscious of the image they project, and unfortunately first impressions are more like first imitations. How a person behaves under adverse circumstances as opposed to favorable ones is not revealed in 30 seconds, but many people are significantly persuaded by first impressions.

Your lover's shopping list not only opens you up to temptation, but the more you are tempted the easier you can be persuaded. Therefore, you have to allow the genuineness of a person to be tested beyond first impressions. In place of the bite size summary at the end of each chapter, I will ask that you complete a few action tasks strategically placed throughout this section, and provide you with a quick shopping guide to assist you with your upcoming shopping experiences. The beauty of each task is that no one can lie to you because you are the only person answering the question or completing the task. Before we anxiously begin picking off someone else's attributes on our fingers and toes, let's step back and allow our own list of vulnerabilities to protect us from landing a spot on someone else's sucker list.

It is not realistic to ask anyone to throw away his or her lover's shopping list altogether because attributes do matter. So, let's gain the advantage by making it our first task. In each task we will integrate several ideas that have been presented thus far, including the fact that trust has to be earned; along with the three-fold test of setting boundaries, observing behavior and communication. Before continuing to the next chapter, show some love to yourself and take this time to complete your first action task.

Action Task #1

Make a list and check it twice

- **First, make a list of the attributes you want in a mate.** Be sure to include any and everything you think you may want in a mate, especially those things that make you weak in the knees, whether they are mental, spiritual or physical attributes. Everyone has a set of things he or she wants to hear or have done, so also include on your list what you want someone to say to you or to do for you. It is important to know what these things are so they do not distort your good judgment when they happen.

- **Second, review your list and rank each item in order of importance.** This is how you expose your vulnerabilities to yourself. Place the focus on you instead of the other person since you are less likely to doubt someone who is doing and saying everything you want. Knowing your vulnerabilities will combat the "tell them what they want to hear" game.
- **Third, add the following two questions to the top of your list.** "Does the person value the truth" and "what is his or her vision for life?" These are two questions you can't definitively answer in a day. The best way to answer these questions is to set boundaries, observe behavior and compare what's communicated to what's actually done. These are questions you may ask directly, but can only be discerned over time. Remember, you are taking those attractive attributes out of your head and

putting them on paper, so that you can visualize what your vulnerabilities are. Here is an example of what your list might look like.

- ✓ Does he or she value the truth?
- ✓ What is his or her vision for life?

1. Intelligent
2. In-shape
3. Tall
4. Godly
5. Outgoing
6. Treats me special
7. Sensitive
8. Loves kids
9. Tells me I'm beautiful
10. Spends money on me
11. Affectionate, etc.

Window Shopping

Is it enough to make an informed decision?

Chapter 8

WINDOW SHOPPING

Acquaintance

Now that you have completed the first task, your list should take on the dual purpose of identifying what you would like in a mate while also exposing your vulnerabilities. This will help you move pass the flattery of attraction and focus on the heart of a person. Awareness of your vulnerabilities is a core regiment of defense against the culture of the game. Awareness is how we take off the blinders that distort our ability to see clearly through the windows of life. The first phase of any relationship is making someone's acquaintance, which is a lot like window shopping. The entire world can be compared to an enormous mall, and every place you go is a department store of potential mates. Window shopping can be a fun and inexpensive way to shop for what you like and dislike or to collect inspiration for what you want. Finding a potential mate in our culture is similar to finding that perfect shirt, dress, or chair. When window shopping, you imagine how the shirt would look on, or if you could live with that chair in your house, but once you buy either product, the appearance is not as important as how well it measures up to your expectations.

Window shopping alone does not tell you whether a pair of pants will fit your curves, or if a shirt will lay just right over your shoulders. You need more information than what is being displayed in order to test the perceived satisfaction of the merchandise. You do not know if that particular product would work for you, all you know is that it looks good in the window. You have to go into the store in order to experience a deeper level of interaction. To get an idea of how the fabric will behave, you must examine it closely and even try it on. When you take a look at yourself in the mirror, the clothing must speak to your sense of style and not just the current trends; how it wears will communicate a special sense of comfort. If you are conservative, it must not push your appearance boundaries, and most importantly, the care instructions communicated on the tag helps you decide if the product will work with your lifestyle.

Such is the case with an acquaintance. It is extremely unlikely that your needs, and the needs of others, will be determined in the acquaintance phase. In the same way that material merchandise does not know that you are checking it out, the average acquaintance is not aware that you are checking him or her out. This means that anyone, regardless of relational status, can go on a window shopping journey and secretly admire the attributes of others. We have all eyed someone's physical attributes at some point, which is how we formulated our infamous list, but just as window shopping is not enough to make an informed purchase, physical attributes are not enough to justify a life long relationship commitment. We have to remind ourselves that liking someone we just met can be an instant response, but trust is one of the many needs of a successful relationship that is earned over time.

Similar to window shopping, making someone's acquaintance is an activity that is never hurried and can happen at just about any point, whether during lunch hour or while standing in line at a local grocery store. The problem is that many people spend little time getting acquainted because the lure of physical attraction is so overpowering. Psychologists at the University of Pennsylvania studied data from over 10,000 speed daters and found that most people make a decision regarding a person's attractiveness within three seconds of meeting.[30] On average, daters will kiss on the second date. [31] And couples have sex within about four to six dates. [32] Anyone who has dated only four to six times is merely acquaintances; but that has not stopped people from sleeping with someone they know little about. What amazes me is that the average person would not open a joint checking account with an acquaintance, but would open their legs to an acquaintance. Of the many things that are being sold in our culture, one thing is for sure; money is more valued than sexual purity. Since people freely exchange sex and sexuality for money, it makes sex one of the largest money making industries in the world.

Although the average acquaintance is not eager to share the intimate details of his or her life on the first date, you have to agree that many are very eager to share sex as soon as possible. I found this to be true even in the biblical story of Samson and Delilah. Samson was persuaded by several acquaintances that he knew little about and was ultimately deceived into a death trap. After making life threatening bets with strangers, wrongfully killing thirty innocent men, stealing their clothes to pay his debt, and sleeping with several prostitutes, Samson eventually lost his life because of the physical attraction he had for Delilah. Here was a powerful man who killed one thousand Philistines with the jawbone of a donkey, escaped Gaza by tearing the gate off the city, and killed a lion with his bare hands, but he did not discern the game, thereby trusting an acquaintance with his most intimate information, the secret to his strength. Basically, Delilah was paid 5,500 pieces of silver to seduce Samson to death.[33] Even then money was more valuable than sexual purity, and Samson lost his life all because he put too much trust into an acquaintance relationship that was motivated by money and sex.

This story should express just how important our relationships are. People can take you up or bring you down. Take control of who you let into your life because you are your most valuable asset. Do not leave your relationships to chance. The AFIEM approach is an excellent way to take control of your relationships and protect yourself against the culture of the game. When dishonest people see that you are not budging on your boundaries, very observant of behavior and are eager to communicate, they will not waste their time and energy playing games with you. Ultimately, that is exactly what you want to happen, because the person who really does not have time for playing games is you.

Taking relationships in phases works because each phase forces you to communicate your way forward. One can not go from being an acquaintance to being a friend without communicating. Phases are indeed the return policy for your relationships. As you compare what is communicated to what is done, you are actually testing behavior. If a person's action does not match his or her words, why would you want that person as a friend? That is where the return policy kicks in; if the friendship does not develop, you can return to being a lifelong acquaintance. A friend should mean you no harm, but one who talks a good game and never follows through is worse than false advertising. When you meet an acquaintance you really do not know how far that relationship will progress, but as long as you set boundaries, observe behavior, and communicate at the beginning of each phase, you can return a relationship to a previous phase before anyone suffers too much wear and tear.

In short, anyone who does not have the level of intimacy that exists in a basic friendship is simply an acquaintance. If you have come into frequent social contact with a person but can not remember his or her name, the person is an acquaintance. One can even become familiar with another through frequent encounters, but until a friendship is established, that person is still just an acquaintance. If liking someone can be an instant response, it is very important to allow a friendship to anchor your relationship so that your eyesight does not get in the way of your foresight. Just like Samson, it is very easy to get caught up in a fantasy world when we are consumed by our list of vulnerabilities, "first imitations," and personal fulfillment objectives, instead of the reality of a progressive relationship. If you take the AFIEM approach seriously your relationship will not be a 'hit or miss' process, but one that inspires friendship, preserves your body and soul, and positions your spirit to rightly discern the truth. When it comes to acquaintance relationships there are just too many things you do not know, so avoid coupling off and becoming exclusive in this phase. Take a lesson from what it truly means to window shop; stay outside the store during the acquaintance phase and you will be less likely to take something back that was bought on impulse.

SHOPPING GUIDE
What to look for in the ACQUAINTANCE department

- **Hours of operation:** Set boundaries; how else will you know when they are being broken.
- **Free Samples:** Do not give too much information in the acquaintance phase. It should be just enough to give someone a taste of what you are about.
- **How may I help you:** Ask open-ended questions that begin with "what," "how" and "why?" Follow up with questions such as "Like what?" "Give me an example..." or "What do you mean by that?" in order to facilitate detailed conversation.
- **No Hassle no haggle:** Do not talk about physical, emotional or sexual intimacy with an acquaintance.
- **Your size:** Engage in spiritual and intellectual discussions that include a comparison of your life goals. If it does not fit put it back.
- **For display only:** Do not allow an acquaintance to invade your personal space by touching your body without approval. This is usually done to gauge how far you will allow the person to go sexually.
- **Great customer service:** Without playing games, you should always seek to preserve the other person while bringing out the best in that person.

Impulse Buying

Couldn't it have waited?

Chapter 9

IMPULSE BUYING

Friendship

After you have encountered someone as an acquaintance, the next and most important phase should always be friendship. As you consider entering the friendship phase, each person should have passed my three-fold test as described in the acquaintance phase: Your boundaries must have been well respected, observed behavior has been acceptable, and the communication lines are open. Friendship is the phase where you share common interests, activities, and concerns with someone who has passed this three-fold test, proving they are ready to move on to a deeper relationship. The friendship phase has growth levels within it and will progress from a casual friendship to a close friendship, and possibly to a best friend relationship. However, the initial desire for a friendship exists because you have spent the appropriate amount of time establishing some essential elements of success. Such elements include but are not limited to the following:

- **Getting to know a person's heart:** Your conversation should move from general to specific questions as you determine that the friendship is working.
- **Accepting one another for who you are:** This is determined by whether or not the two of you embraces each other's uniqueness, differences, and imperfections.
- **Committing to sharing time:** If a person does not have time to be your friend, but has time to make out with you, it is very likely that the relationship will end painfully. Both involved must give of his or her time in order to establish a friendship.
- **Trustworthiness and Honesty:** These two qualities are very similar; however, the only difference I want to advocate is the order in which one comes to this conclusion. Just because a person seems honest does not make the person worthy of your trust. Trustworthiness is what earns a person the distinction of being regarded as honest. Do not jump to any honesty conclusions until trustworthiness has been tested.

- **Forgiving**: We all make mistakes. Forgiveness is important because the goal is not to find a friend who is perfect, but to find one who is not playing any games. I often forgive my current friends without them ever knowing that I was offended.
- **Spiritual agreement:** Can you talk to the person about your beliefs? Imagine being friends with someone and the most intimate area of your life is off limits because that person does not agree with what you believe. This is why friendship is the most important phase. Because it lays a foundation based on these essential elements of success, which adds substance to a relationship long before it becomes intimately exclusive.

These are all essential elements that help determine if going to the next phase is even an option. Many people make the huge mistake of skipping the friendship phase altogether and move blindly into an exclusive relationship, only to find out too late that the aforementioned essential elements do not exist. Maybe they are more consumed with the idea of losing a short-term sex partner than gaining a long-term friend. Maybe the emphasis gets shifted to becoming an exclusive dating couple, where two acquaintances who really do not know the other spend a sexual season together only to confirm that once the passion has died there is nothing left to support the relationship. I like to compare this behavior to impulse buying because emotions and feelings play a decisive role in why people skip over friendship and move quickly into intimacy. It feels as though you've got to have it, but when you get it home, similar to impulse buying, you realize it was just an irrational and emotional response that could have waited.

Often, when we are led by our emotions they result in feelings of guilt or disappointment to say the least. For instance, when you see a gorgeous dress or a bodacious big screen TV, emotions can be triggered, and depending on how it is advertised, it can cause you to purchase a product only to have buyer's remorse shortly after. These same emotions can be triggered when you encounter an attractive person who is dressed well, nicely groomed, and who has his or her assets displayed perfectly. Such attraction can cause one to see a person like you would see a promotional product that screams "Forget just being a friend I want more!" when actually without friendship you are getting much less than you could have ever bargained for.

Even if you are playing games on purpose and see someone as just another attractive sexual notch under your belt, all people involved are subject to losing something. The more intimate you become with a person the harder it is to remove the pain, scars, and emotional ties when you finally realize that what you got was not worth what you gave up. Obviously, people carry these past experiences into their next relationship, thickening the strand of unresolved issues that eventually weaves an intricate web of failed relationships.

Many people never heal from past hurt and pain before jumping into their next relationship. When the past hurt of one combines with the pain of another, the effects can become compounded, making settling down with one person feel more like a tremendous risk and marriage like the ultimate gamble. They realize that past experiences have shaped their current thinking as they ask themselves, *"What if he turns out like my deadbeat dad and leaves me to raise my kids all by myself? What if he secretly molests my kids, like my dad molested me? What if she is a shopaholic and can't be trusted with money like my mother was? What if she is pure evil wrapped in a smile just like my ex-wife?"* These thoughts act like invisible webbing that has weaved mental, emotional and sexual barriers to a successful relationship.

This intricate web of confusion has been spun from so many mental, emotional, and sexual angles that it becomes challenging to be satisfied with just one person, which contributes to why many couples are primed to fail in a marriage relationship. The unfortunate reality is that marriage is where many of these mental, emotional, and sexual cobwebs become frighteningly visible. And instead of putting in the work required to remove the cobwebs, many people opt to divorce or simply move from one relationship to the next weaving new webs into the fabric of their relational existence.

When the average couple refuses to do anything about the negative effects of their unresolved issues, the growing divorce rate is inevitable. One source even reported on the economic consequences of divorce stating that it causes a 73 percent decline in women's standards of living.[34]

Divorce also contributes to why fathers have greatly decreased their involvement in childrearing and why many siblings do not grow up together. Without going any further, these are enough losses to conclude that when playing games one may lose less, but no one ever wins because we have devalued the friendship phase and trained ourselves to move quickly into a sexually intimate relationship.

In the traditional dating culture people often skip over the friendship phase as if it has no value or think it will automatically happen when two people enter an exclusive dating relationship. This is evident through the use of such cultural terms as boyfriend and girlfriend, but one may ask is that boy or girl really your friend? Many dating relationships end with someone saying, "Maybe we should just be friends", but since a friendship was never established, just being friends never works. Many have confused friendship with whatever they were doing. Do not confuse friendship with becoming exclusive with someone, because these are two different phases of a relationship. Knowing what phase you are in at all times will help set realistic expectations and eliminate the confusion, frustration, and hurt. The friendship phase should continue to build trust and not lust, so that the proper time and value can be placed on the friendship. Whenever I speak on this topic I always get the most feedback when I present the following three **wrong** reasons to date exclusively:

1. **Do not date to have fun:** If you become exclusive with someone only to have fun, settling down with one person for life will feel like your source of fun is being eliminated, which is not true. The rush that you get from meeting someone new can condition you to want someone new for no other reason than how exciting the experience is. People play games daily in the name of fun, but when the fun ceases to exist, they move on to someone different in order to reignite that rush. Do not let the rush of being with someone new lure you into the culture of the game. Train yourself to have fun "with" people and not at the "expense" of people.

2. **Do not date to find a mate:** This is dangerously deceptive because there is no way you can date all the men or women that would interest you while separating yourself from the mental and emotional baggage that comes with it. One of the top qualities most people want in a mate is loyalty. The average person you date will not want to share you with others, making it very tricky to date more than one person at a time. Therefore, it will be difficult for you to know when you have found the right person if you have not even scratched the surface of potential people to date? For those who believe that the best way to find a mate is to date, then why waste your time dating one person at a time? Why not date one-hundred and one people at a time if your goal is to find a mate? I guarantee that if you do find a mate through dating numerous people, the leftover residue from the mental and emotional ties will prove how strong a hold it has on your soul.

You will literally develop the urge to never settle down with just one person.

3. **Do not date to build commitment:** This is another dangerous deception because a person's will is involved. How do you know for sure when someone is committed to you? Is commitment confirmed by the things a person has done for you? Have you ever experienced what I call the "after all I've done for you" syndrome in the midst of a break-up? This tactic is a person's attempt to remind another that everything he or she did while dating was done to build commitment. You should not commit to someone that is obviously not right for you simply because of how much the person has done for you. This is why dating to build commitment does not work. You may not want to commit to a person once you get to know the person better and visa versa. Remember, the three-fold test can measure commitment in each phase of AFIEM.

When it comes to commitment, it has to be all or nothing. Two out of three is bad. Three out of three is commitment. The only thing that changes about the test is what you are adding to your commitment as you progress from one phase to the next. The above explanations of those wrong reasons usually lead into the second most popular question that I suspect you are asking yourself right now. "How will I know what I want in a mate if I don't date?" Well, here again is where one must denounce the culture of the game, which works to conform our thinking to its lowest possible standards. Instead of dating to have fun, to find a mate, or to build commitment, try dating to build friendship? After all this is what straight people do with their same sex friends. When my guy friends got married, I told their wives that they were getting good men. I came to that conclusion because of the friendship I have with their husbands, not because I have exclusively "dated" their husbands. In the same way, people of the opposite sex can date to build friendship. The beauty of dating this way is that one of two things will happen; either you will gain a friend for life, or you will marry your very best friend. That is what I call a win-win situation.

The typical dating couple, however, does not focus on these kinds of results until their baggage of pain is just about filled to capacity. This action occurs mainly because this concept requires taking the high road and re-thinking what it really means to go on a date with someone. For example, I have never met a couple who concluded that they were dating exclusively long before ever going on a first date. Usually the traditional first date is just to find out if you even want to see that person again! If we change our view of a date to that of a social appointment, or a period of time arranged between people with no strings attached, then it would be much easier to focus on building friendship. When the focus is to build friendship, not only can you go on dates with as many people as you want at one time, but this focus will change why you date as well as who you date.

If you could get a truthful answer from the typical guy, he would tell you that he sees himself dating someone he wants to have sex with, but not so much someone he wants to be friends with. The irony is that most people would not want to spend their life with someone who is not their friend. A life mate is supposed to be your friend more than anyone else. In every relationship turbulent storms will come, and during those times the goo-goo eyes, sexual passion, and overly *amorous* conversation that got you where you are, will eventually shatter under all the pressure. Heated moments of passion will no longer support your foundation, and the relationship will begin to freefall from the high point that it once floated.

Do not get me wrong, I am not trying to burst your bubble. I am simply trying to help you understand that if you neglected the friendship phase of your relationship, returning to that phase is where you will find your best hope. As your relationship is freefalling it may seem hopeless, but true friendship can work even in the midst of a storm. Remember, with AFIEM you can always revert back to a previous phase. So if your relationship has spiraled out of control, go ahead and stretch out your hand of friendship, and I guarantee you will find that friendship was indeed that practical substance you were missing.

SHOPPING GUIDE
What to look for in the FRIENDSHIP department

- **Avoid door to door salesman:** Do not involve yourself sexually with someone you are getting to know as a friend. Friends with benefits should have nothing to do with sex.
- **The Return Policy:** To avoid impulse buying, as you consider entering the friendship phase, each person should have passed the three-fold test of respecting boundaries, having acceptable behavior and open to communication. If they fail this test, take them back to the acquaintance phase.
- **No Commission:** If a person does not have time to be your friend, but has time to make out with you, it is very likely that you are not the only one, and the relationship will eventually end painfully.
- **The Quality Inspection:** A friendship should have at least six essential elements for success: Getting to know the heart, Acceptance, Commitment of time, Trustworthiness/honesty, Forgiveness, Spiritual agreement;
- **Credit Worthiness:** Do not let anyone who is obviously not right for you cash in on your commitment simply because of how much they have done for you. Instead of dating to have fun, to find a mate, or to build commitment, try dating to build friendship. A Good Friendship is your credit.

Specialty Goods

Why exactly are you in such high demand?

Chapter 10

SPECIALTY GOODS

Intimacy

If the friendship phase is about building trust, then the intimacy phase should be about determining whether the two of you want to build a life together. By moving respectfully into an authentic friendship, you are able to increase your ability to discern the game based on real life situations. You are convinced that the person has been a trustworthy friend and is not out to play games. You have tested behavior within certain boundaries and now feel safe enough to communicate on a more intimate level. The person has achieved high results on the three-fold test, and now it is safe to explore whether moving into an exclusive relationship is mutual. What a breath of fresh air it is when two hearts that know each other consider moving from friendship to intimate sharing. How refreshing is the idea of sharing your intimate thoughts with someone who accepts you for who you are, someone who has given their time to you as a friend, someone who has earned your trust, someone who is forgiving of your mistakes, and someone who connects with your spirit and soul. This person is obviously special, which is why I compare the intimacy phase to shopping for specialty goods.

Specialty goods are items that are extraordinary and unique enough to motivate people to make an unusual effort to get them and keep them. This is where the huge shopping mall of dating dwindles down to just a few uncommon stores where special friends meet. These friends are not only viewed as special, but as limited-editions and stunning works of art. In your eyes they have become the priceless people that you will treasure for the rest of your life. However, only when you follow the process does it become clear to you that a certain person is particularly special. No one could have ever sold you on this person at first glance, but now you can say without a shadow of a doubt that you trust the person; you love the person, and you want this person to be exclusively yours. You have no intentions whatsoever of playing games, but even now you must continue to guide your emotions, because this is the phase where I have seen much of the relational pain take place. Relational pain occurs in this phase not because it is a painful phase, but mainly because people are skipping to this phase prematurely. This means that many of us are becoming intimate with people whom we know little about. Remember, this person is not just someone who wants to know your name; this is someone you are letting into your most special place, your life. Letting someone into your life should be held as a high privilege and never taken for granted.

The intimate sharing phase should be reserved for sharing close personal thoughts with someone you know very well. There should be an extreme level of trust and a mutual understanding of just how special the two of you are to one another. This is why an established friendship is so important, because true intimacy is possible only because of the friendship that comes before it. When my wife and I got married, the sex was there but the intimacy was not because our friendship was non-existent. I remember waking up to the reality that I no longer liked her, and she no longer liked me. It was all because we skipped the most important phase of our relationship. I began to wonder why I never argued with my guy friends or why she never argued with her female friends. It became obvious that the whole focus between the "fellas" was friendship, and the same focus was also between the girls. My wife and I had not yet made friendship a focus in our relationship; therefore, we did not know much about how special we could be to one another.

It has been said that grace is God giving us what we do not deserve, and mercy is God not giving us what we do deserve. In that case, my wife and I were recipients of both grace and mercy. As our marriage was spiraling into a freefall, we reached out our hands of friendship as if we were trying to pull ourselves closer, while resisting the wind and pressure of a treacherous cyclone and we became friends. To say the least, marriage is not the best time to establish a friendship, and many people divorce for lack of being friends because when you hit rock bottom, what you need most is a friend. Earlier I asked the question "what do you believe?" and I will answer that question again by telling you I believe there is hope in God, because even though my wife and I went about marriage wrong, our relationship with God made it right.

This period in my marriage is where our spiritual intimacy with God made all the difference. Not only were we justified of our wrongs, but I do not believe our marriage could have made it without **an intimate relationship with God**. If you really stop and think about intimacy with God, you have to conclude that intimacy is not about having sex. Many people will tell you they have or want an intimate relationship with God, but such intimacy is accomplished through spending time and gaining knowledge of Him. Jesus said take my yoke upon you and learn of me for I am meek and lowly in heart.[35] A yoke is a fitting for the neck that binds two animals together so that one will be in lock step with the other. On the contrary, the yoke of Christ is easy, because it is lined with a love so great that he would lay down his life for his friends.[36] The yoke of Christ personifies intimacy, but here again we can point out the emphasis on friendship that comes before intimacy. When we choose to walk with Christ, talk with Christ, and learn from Christ we can understand just how much of a friend He is. When we accept Christ as friend, it makes it easy to accept Christ as our Lord and Savior, which opens the door for us to have an intimate relationship with Him as God.

Intimacy is a **strong sense of endearment**, and we are so dear to God that he gave his only son so that He could live with us forever. I have learned from my relationship with God that anyone you plan to spend forever with must also share intimacy with one another. The focus of an intimate relationship should be **to bring out the best in the other person**. That is what God did for me. His words are very intimate for those who take them seriously, and the more I learn from Him, the more He brings the best out of me. Actually, I credit the overall success of my marriage to a self-imposed period of time I set aside to ask God to help me with my marriage. Without His wisdom, my marriage would have been just another failed statistic.

Bringing out the best in someone is a challenge, especially when the average person wants the best to already be there. Are you up to the challenge of bringing out the best in one another? Your answer to this question will determine if you are ready to move from the friendship phase to the intimate sharing phase. Once you have an established friendship, this question should be very easy to answer because of the endearment you already have for one another. If you love each other as friends, you make it a point to move forward for two reasons. The first is that this is something you both want; and the second is that both of you are up for the challenge of bringing out the best in one another. The intimacy phase is about living in the reality that no one is perfect while committing to make one another better. Intimacy is where communication gets its chance to shine on center stage because this deeper level of intimate sharing only happens with the person you have agreed to become exclusive with. This is why it is important to talk about becoming exclusive before you actually agree to become exclusive. This will ensure that your decisions are not based on mere emotions.

At this point in the process, it is ok to communicate what you are feeling because you are communicating with an established friend. Both of you should be in agreement with moving the friendship to the next level, and because you have an established friendship, it will be easier to hear "NO" and accept it. If you are guided by your emotions, "NO" will not feel good because your emotions often linger on, knocking at a closed door even though the person is metaphorically not there. However, if you take control and guide your emotions, when you find yourself knocking at the door of intimacy and it does not open, all you have to do is remain friends. Naturally, you will have a few minor emotions to overcome, but you will not become the proverbial fly in the emotional web that eventually gets the life sucked right out of it. You actually have a much better chance of maintaining the friendship. I must add that if one person wants to remain friends, then the other should not try to coerce the relationship into a deeper level of intimacy. Intimate sharing between friends works best when it is a mutual agreement. If you have a special friendship with someone that has passed the three-fold test and both of you are ready to move to the intimate sharing phase, then you truly have something special working to your advantage.

Another real advantage of the AFIEM approach is that it helps to remove our greatest fear, the fear of rejection. As you move from one phase to the next by guiding your emotions, the fear of rejection will be minimized because you are dealing with an established friend. By the time a relationship progresses to the marriage phase, the fear of rejection should be totally removed because ultimately that is what our marriage vows are supposed to accomplish. Think about the words "till death do us part." When we profess these words openly we are actually removing the fear of rejection. One can not have intimacy with a person until the fear of rejection is removed. If rejection is our greatest fear, then love has to be the greater force that drives out fear. I believe God spoke the words "I will never leave you or forsake you," because He knew He had to drive out the fear of rejection before we could have an intimate relationship with Him. When we say the marriage vow, "till death do us part," we are actually saying I will never leave you or forsake you. I know many people today are not proponents of marriage, but I know for myself that there is an even deeper level of intimacy that can only be achieved in marriage because the God of love Himself came up with the whole idea.

We need the love of God so that those of us who believe there is a judgment can stand boldly without fear of rejection. I like to think of it this way-- if I was accused of a crime and all evidence pointed to my guilt, I would have fear when it was time for me to face the judge. Since God is my judge in eternity, I rest on his word that says, "Love has been made perfect among us in this: that we may have boldness in the Day of Judgment."[37] I have no fear of that Day of Judgment because God also said, "I will never leave you or forsake you."[38] Fear has to do with punishment, but love has to do with reward. Even though I was guilty, God's love moved me into an intimate relationship with Him that is filled with rewards; one of which is total vindication. I am a friend of God, and just as it is rewarding for me to have an intimate relationship with my heavenly friend, so is it rewarding for two loving friends to move into an intimate relationship with one another here on earth. With that in mind, here are a couple of things that I believe should be reserved for the intimate sharing phase.

- **Grooming:** Ladies this is where you can fix us up, dress us up, and clean us up. This is where you get the unique opportunity to make us better, because the average guy really can not accept a random woman's criticism. However, your friendship should be so strong at this point that he welcomes a little constructive criticism. But as you load him up with your improvement advice; remember to lift him up by saying it in the most respectful way. No matter what phase of the relationship we are in as men we will always have a need to feel respected.

Think of grooming as putting the icing on the cake, not making the cake.

- **Pre-marital Counseling:** It is unconventional to even think about pre-marital counseling before there is a proposal, but this is a great way to keep the communication lines open. Why wait until you are engaged and the wedding date is set to attend pre-marital counseling? What if you find out something in counseling that needs to be addressed before marriage? The ideal time to receive this counseling is now. This is no longer just dinner and a movie. Pre-marital counseling will stir a more intimate conversation. If you see the person as a potential life mate then you need to be able to see the light at the end of the tunnel before you travel down that road. Pre-marital counseling can reveal that light, or it may reveal that there is no light at all. If the right kind of intimacy exists it will lead you into the next phase of engagement or confirm what should remain a friendship for life.

We have already discussed the fact that true intimacy exists without sex. Therefore, sex should not be your topic of discussion in the intimacy phase. Intimacy should be your topic of discussion because it is possible to have sex without any form of intimacy. Intimacy has to do with the amount of mental peace, emotional peace, physical peace, social peace, financial peace, and most importantly, the spiritual peace that exist in the relationship. Each of these factors plays a part in creating levels of intimacy that literally have no end. Intimate sharing is where two friends who value the truth can open their hearts to one another without sexual interference or emotional intoxication. Your soul is not tied to sex; it is tied to the friendship, and that truth alone will protect you from the culture of the game.

Sexual intimacy only teaches you the strength of urges, desires, and physical attraction. I am pretty sure you do not need the intimacy phase to teach you another lesson about how strong sexual urges can be. We have learned that lesson from the culture of the game. If the urge to become sexual in this phase becomes uncontrollable, it is because you are talking about and doing things that fuel sexual urges instead of the factors of peace that create intimacy. People who agree to share this kind of intimacy do not come a dime a dozen. They are like uncommon specialty goods no longer found in the common store. They have no intentions of playing games and are willing to pay the price for that special someone.

SHOPPING GUIDE

What to expect in the INTIMACY department

- **Customer loyalty:** Intimacy is a strong sense of endearment that requires a close, familiar, and loving personal friendship with someone who has passed the three-fold test in both the acquaintance and friendship phases.
- **Victory's Secret:** Intimate sharing is where two friends who value the truth, can open their hearts to one another without sexual interference or emotional intoxication.
- **One Size does not fit all:** There should be an extreme level of trust and a mutual understanding of just how special the two of you are to one another. If one person wants to remain friends, then the other should not try to coerce the relationship into intimacy.
- **A Private Fitting Room:** Sex should not be the focus of intimacy. Bringing out the best in the other person should be your focus. Otherwise, do not move into the intimate sharing phase.
- **The Naked Truth:** Intimacy is where communication gets its chance to shine on center stage, as this deeper level of sharing happens only with the person you have agreed to become exclusive with.

Precious Gems

The question is: how do you see yourself?

Chapter 11

PRECIOUS GEMS

Engagement

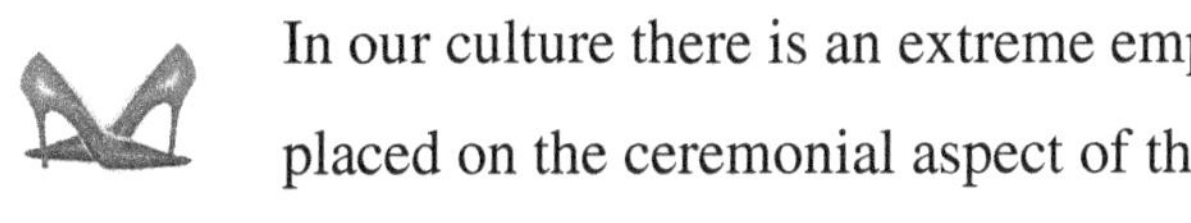

In our culture there is an extreme emphasis placed on the ceremonial aspect of the marriage relationship. Everything leading up to this big event has to be perfect even if the big event is a small court house wedding. According to the National Association of Wedding Ministers, the average American engagement is sixteen months, and the average amount spent on a traditional American wedding is $22,000. My wife and I did not spend nearly that much on our wedding. I would like to think maybe that is why we did not fall within the statistic that the average newly-married couple only has about $1,000 in savings, but of course it takes a little more financial savvy than staying within a wedding budget. Could it be that finances are the number one topic that married couples fight about because we have spent all our money on our weddings? Avoiding spending all our money on our wedding is one of the few things my wife and I got right. We outlined our wedding budget and together we saved to pay cash for every aspect, including the honeymoon. Although, we cut out many of the wedding and pre-wedding customs that did not fit our budget, the engagement ring was one of the few customs that I took very seriously.

Engagement is usually marked by the man presenting the woman with a precious stone. One part is given as an engagement ring when she accepts the marriage proposal and the other during the wedding ceremony. On a small scale, it is a symbol of how greatly valued and highly prized a woman is to her bridegroom. This is a man's most symbolic gesture that distinguishes a woman to be his exclusive treasure for life. Just as the ring is set with precious gems that command a premium price in the market due to its extraordinary brilliance and rarity, every woman is unique as a precious gem in the eyes of her true beholder.

When a man prepares to move into the engagement phase of a relationship, he is looking to woo the one person who will become his most precious gem. As he steps into the bedazzling jewelry store of life, all the energy of his inner circle becomes directed towards helping him seal the deal on the one special relationship phase we call engagement. For the men who are married, do you remember all the support your inner circle gave you to make your proposal as special as possible? Everyone was in on it and wanted to share that special moment along with you. I remember the support I received, as well as the support I have given to others. And no matter how dark the statistical cloud of divorce becomes, we all share one common hope that the giving of a ring will be accompanied by a silver lining which embodies everything beautiful in a marriage relationship.

As a couple progresses to the engagement phase, boundaries will become more relaxed but should remain somewhere within the yellow and green caution points until the promise to marry is fulfilled. After all, engagement is a promise, but playing games can make it feel more like a problem. Some men are hesitant to get engaged because they are unsure about this promise to marry. Others are uncomfortable with change or have a fear of the unknown. Some are looking for the perfect fantasy relationship that really does not exist. And others think they are going to miss out on their chance to marry America's next top model. Trust me, I am a guy, and I know that the true underlying issue that makes men hesitant is our own personal struggles that have little or nothing to do with the woman at hand.

This is why many men enjoy being a long-term boyfriend, but is doubtful of becoming a long-term husband. Women, on the other hand, seem to enjoy being long term wives, but dread becoming a long-term girlfriend. Consequently, men seem to have more issues before marriage that only God knows, and women seem to have more issues after marriage that only God knows. And quite frankly no matter what is said or done, the issues are often issues that only God can resolve.

Relationally, we are single, engaged, or married, and there is continuous learning in all three states respectively. However, engagement seems to be the relational state where the least amount of learning takes place. It is as though the engagement phase is simply the period of time designated for planning the wedding, but there is so much more to learn in this phase. Engagement is the same word as the biblical term betrothal, which also means a promise to marry. In biblical days this was a formal contract considered just as binding as marriage today, and a divorce was required to terminate a betrothal. Think about it; when a man gets down on one knee and asks a woman to marry him, he does not ask, "Will you engage me?" He asks, "Will you marry me?" And all who witnesses the proposal are certain to let out a hopeful cheer when she exhales in nervous excitement "Yes! Yes!" Although the engagement comes with the asking, there are times when the engagement ring does not come until later. This is definitely a time for the suspecting audience to let out a resounding "Boo! Boo!"

Ladies, when a man asks you to marry him, I urge you to make him "bring the bling!" Do not go to the next phase of engagement without a relatively expensive ring on your finger! Also, keep in mind that he did not let you borrow the ring; he gave it to you and asked you to marry him. If it does not work out, you should keep the ring! Do not let your will get in the way of the deal! When men start losing enough expensive rings that alone will make us stop playing and start praying! However, there is one exception; if you break it off with him it is only fair to give the ring back.

I have learned some pretty convincing lessons from reading about Joseph and Mary's engagement. They were the earthly parents of the one and only Jesus Christ who became the source of our eternal salvation. Mary was pregnant with Jesus during her engagement to Joseph, and the bible says this happened before they ever came together.[39] This word together in the Greek basically means conjugal cohabitation.[40] Therefore, not only did Joseph abstain from sex with Mary, but neither did they live together or spend erotic time together. This is how Joseph knew for sure that he did not impregnate Mary when she was found with child of the Holy Spirit. Therefore, Joseph, who is virtually Mary's husband at this point and being a just man who kept the law, could have made a public example out of Mary by taking her out in the street to be stoned to death, or burned.[41] Instead, Joseph continued to have Mary's best interest in mind, so he decided to secretly give her a bill of divorce before two witnesses, which was also one of his legal options.

If you and your fiancé were abstaining from sex, but somehow a baby was born with someone else, you would be furious right? You would be furious even if you were not abstaining. Not only would your trust have been betrayed, but a virtual promise would have been broken; therefore, the engagement would have been off. I believe Joseph also concluded that Mary had violated a contractual agreement by having sex with someone else. Since betrothal was like a contractual agreement, Joseph had to make a move that was within the law. But after he had narrowed it down to divorce, an angel of the Lord appeared to him in a dream and said, "Joseph son of David, don't be afraid to take Mary home as your wife, because what is conceived in her is from the Holy Spirit. She will give birth to a son, and you are to give him the name Jesus, because he will save his people from their sins."[42] This shows the kind of relationship Joseph had with God because he accepted those words to be truth and was thereby compelled to protect and preserve Mary so that Jesus would be born of a virgin, and Mary would become the most reverent mother in the history of mankind.

Think about the honor that God placed on virginity. Does this open your eyes to any other social debates? Jesus was born of a virgin, but not just any virgin, this virgin was virtually married in God's eyes. That is why the angels had to intervene because Joseph was about to divorce Mary. God could have chosen to bring His son through an unmarried virgin, or a virgin who would never marry, but I believe this is a testament to the honor God places on marriage when it comes to having children. God told Joseph to take Mary home, and he thereby places the highest endorsement upon marriage and family that exists today. Jesus Christ, God's only begotten son, was born into a fully functional, model family that included a husband and a wife. This model is consistently held in high esteem throughout the bible.

None of us can compare our relationship to what happened to Joseph and Mary, but we can learn a lot from Joseph's relationship with God the Father. By no means do I compare my wife's father to God, but I do understand the freedom her father's endorsement provided to us. On the day that I asked him for his daughter's hand in marriage, I told him that I had done what he had asked me to do concerning his daughter. His words to me were, "she is your responsibility now," as he shook my hand. In other words, "take her home with you." No matter how it comes, a father's endorsement is refreshingly relieving. It was as if his endorsement consummated our engagement and gave us permission to build a family and life together that included him. Others of you may already have kids from a previous relationship and are looking not only for a father's endorsement, but also an endorsement from your kids. Regardless of your situation, whether you are single with no kids or coming together as a blended family, it is very important that all of you understand and accept each other's pre-existing family structure to help make your relationship a success.

Joseph and Mary's example also confirms that engagement does not have to be an emotional decision made alone. When you are open to hear from God, you are able to make a clear and wise decision. Joseph was considered to be a just man and Mary was considered *virtuous* because of their relationships with God. When you seek to bring out the best in each other, it does not stop when you get engaged. The best should be yet to come, as each phase of the AFIEM approach is intended to collect wisdom along the way that will pay off in marriage, which is ultimately the most honorable phase of them all.

SHOPPING GUIDE
What to look for in the ENGAGEMENT department

- **Be dazzled:** Just as the engagement ring houses precious gems that command a premium price in the market due to its extraordinary brilliance and rarity, every woman is unique as a precious gem in the eyes of her true beholder.
- **Cut-Clarity-Color:** This has nothing to do with body type, complexion or ethnic background, but everything to do with making him "bring the bling!" Ladies, do not go to the next phase of engagement without a relatively expensive ring on your finger. Period!
- **Solitaire or Baguettes:** Whether you are single with no kids or coming together as a blended family, it is very important that each of you understand and accept each other's pre-existing family structure to help make your relationship a success. Marriage is a family covenant.
- **The Setting:** Although engaged couples do not have the green light yet, your boundaries in the engagement phase will become more relaxed as the relationship progresses. However, you should still relate somewhere within the yellow and green caution points until you make good on your promise to marry.

Exclusive Dealers

Who are you willing to cut off?

Chapter 12

EXCLUSIVE DEALERS

Marriage

You should know by now that the culture of the game does not favor exclusivity, but there are many benefits to becoming exclusive. According to webster.com, "exclusive" means "limited to possession, control, or use by a single individual; excluding others from participation." Real-estate agents, for instance, traditionally offer some form of an Exclusive Buyer Agency Agreement that restricts the buyer from hiring another agent during the home buying process. In business, having an exclusive dealership agreement creates obligation through a contractual relationship between two parties, but in marriage we do not simply sign an expiring contract, we enter into an exclusive agreement with someone we believe will be our lifelong mate. If you understand the words "exclusive," "contract," and "covenant," then you are already familiar with the framework of marriage. However, covenant is probably less understood of the three, since it is a spiritual word with spiritual rules and is therefore subject to spiritual interpretation. When two people grasp the idea of covenant, both the legal and spiritual agreements are combined to make marriage the "super-natural" union that it is.

Although many people today could care less about marriage, it is the essential principle that has brought joy, productivity and stability to our society. Imagine the kind of world it would be if people had not adhered to the covenant of marriage throughout history. Actually, I do not have to do much imagining because I believe it would look much worse than the culture I have described in the first half of this book. Without covenants, contracts, and agreements, the culture of the game would run wild like a ferocious Tasmanian devil feeding on any relationship that crosses its path. Here again, is why applying the three-fold test at every phase of a relationship is so important. Learning to honor boundaries, behave appropriately, and communicate effectively in the early stages of AFIEM will prepare you to do the same in marriage, which is the most exclusive phase in this entire approach.

I must repeat. Anyone can simply live like he or she is married, even without signing an actual contract, but in order to receive the help needed in marriages today, one must embrace covenant. The Hebrew word for covenant is carat, which means "to cut." I find it very symbolic that gem stones have to be cut in order to fit into the setting of a symbolic wedding ring. But what is even more symbolic is how the cutting of hands was an ancient practice which required bloodshed to comingle in order to put a covenant into effect as with David and Jonathan.[43] By shaking hands, the blood would mingle, and a bond was made before God. Covenant is a word God used throughout the bible, particularly regarding His relationship with Israel. The word denoted a spiritual contract made between God and Israel which provides the grounds for a spiritual interpretation of marriage.[44] I can only encourage you to fully embrace covenant as it is the secret to a successful marriage relationship today.

Although some may say that a contract and a covenant are virtually the same, I want to reiterate that a covenant is what makes a natural contract supernatural. According to God there are spiritual terms to a marriage covenant which was symbolized by His marriage to Israel. When a couple signs a natural marriage contract and embraces a spiritual covenant, they are agreeing to add the following supernatural principles to their relationship:

Blood Covenant

God's marriage to Israel was consummated with the bloodshed of an animal sacrifice. Once Israel agreed to God's covenant, Moses sprinkled blood on the people to seal the deal and said, "This is the blood of the covenant that the Lord has made with you in accordance with all these words."[45] Wedding ceremonies that include the exchange of vows before witnesses are similarly important to us in our modern day, but we all know that true sacrifice takes place as those vows are tested in marriage. To sacrifice something means to surrender it or to give it up. A beautiful bride dressed in white is symbolic of purity, as two friends would have waited to sacrifice the seal of their virginity. The idea is that on their honeymoon night, the bride is sexually penetrated for the first time by her trusted husband, breaking the hymen and causing her blood to flow over his penis in the most vivid expression of blood covenant there is. Think about it, there is no deal more exclusive than knowing that your spouse is your first and only partner.

According to data from the national survey of family growth, by age seventeen 95 percent of Americans have had premarital sex, sacrificing our virginity with someone we probably had no intention of marrying. I am willing to bet that people are more cautious about breaking the seal of a fine bottle of wine at just the right moment than they are about breaking the seal of their virginity. Could it be that the occasion for a fine bottle of wine is more special than the occasion for our first sexual experience? My wedding was beautiful, and my wife's and my contract is binding, but how much more could we have become one flesh if we both had waited to break the seal of our virginity in marriage? Even though most of us reading this book will have already sacrificed our virginity, it is not too late; God can still restore this supernatural covenant in our marriage. As my wife and I grew to understand and apply this principle, God honored our prayers and restored our blood covenant relationship. I believe God can restore this blessing in any marriage if couples are willing to submit to His boundaries.

The Covenant Name

When my wife changed her name on paper, it identified her as an added member of the Boswell family, but the more she spoke it as a part of her identity, the more real it became to everyone that heard it. As a matter of fact, both family names became one, as two people from two different families entered into one covenant. We both gained the authority to act on the other's behalf in both legal and business matters, all because we are associated with the same name. This is the type of authority God's covenant name gave to Israel when he said, "Wherever I cause my name to be honored, I will come to you and bless you."[46]

There are many names God used to reveal himself to Israel, but there is one that particularly stood out to me in light of the covenant God made with Israel. That name is "El Olam," which means everlasting God.[47] No wonder God made an everlasting covenant with every living creature of all flesh upon the earth and established His covenant between the seed and their generations.[48] In essence, God made an everlasting covenant with Israel that did not die, but is still offered to every believer today because God is everlasting. The seed of covenant originated with God, therefore making it a spiritual seed because God is a spirit. Covenant is not at all a natural contract that we sign, but rather a spiritual agreement that we speak. When I said, "I take this woman to be my wife, to have and to hold from this day forward, for better or for worse, for richer, for poorer, in sickness and in health, to love and to cherish; until death do us part," and began introducing her as Mrs. Boswell, those words produced a sense of oneness that can never be achieved through a signature alone. Every time we speak our name, Mr. and Mrs. Boswell, we are speaking in both natural contract and spiritual covenant, hence the super-natural. And there is nothing anyone can do to experience the spiritual blessing of marriage, except embrace God's covenant.

The Covenant Table

A happy nuclear family is notable for sharing day to day eating at a family table, but eating together has also become a central part of social relationships. Sharing a table of food is a universal method of expressing fellowship with another. It is an opportunity to communicate, strengthen friendship bonds, and come together. However, when God's covenant was confirmed with Israel, the entire family was represented. Moses got up early the next morning and built an altar at the foot of the mountain of God and set up twelve stone pillars representing the twelve tribes of Israel. More young Israelite men were then sent to offer burnt offerings and sacrifice animals as fellowship offerings to the Lord. When God invited Moses, Aaron, Nadab, Abihu and seventy of the elders of Israel to come up to Him and worship, God did not raise his hand against these leaders; they all saw God, and they all ate and drank from the table.[49]

Marriage is covenant, and just as God requires friendship and total forgiveness before He enters into covenant with us, we must allow friendship and total forgiveness to exist in our natural relationships. Moses built an altar so that sacrifices could be placed on it, which allowed God's forgiveness.[50] Do you find it interesting that weddings are referred to as going to the altar? A wedding couple should choose to forgive because once you are married it is very hard to enjoy the designated family dining table with un-forgiveness towards your covenant partner.

It is also important to understand that when two people enter the covenant of marriage, the two extended families become one. The twelve pillars that were erected represented the other parties to the covenant. Moses had to pass these pillars to get to the altar. In the same way, we have to acknowledge the fact that we are not just entering into covenant with our spouses, we are also entering into covenant with both sides of the family. Think of the extended family at the wedding who sits on either side as pillars of support that have come no longer to offer a dead animal sacrifice but to offer themselves as living sacrifices. Two lives and two families will become one. Now God's written word should resonate with you a lot stronger where it says "Behold the blood of the covenant."[51] Blood covenant is a supernatural exchange. The one and only sacrifice of His Son initiated a perpetual covenant of promises that can restore, establish, and empower marriages today. Understand that whether we choose marriage covenant or not, God has offered to us the chance to be a covenant people by the blood sacrifice of Jesus.

You should now be familiar with the five phases of AFIEM, but before concluding, I want to keep my promise of dedicating a chapter to the subject of sex inside of marriage. After all, if you really want to put this approach into practice, sex outside of marriage will become some of what you communicate, one of your boundaries, and none of your behavior.

SHOPPING GUIDE

What to look for in the MARRIAGE department

- **Catering to self**: I am willing to bet that people are more cautious about breaking the seal of a fine bottle of wine at just the right moment than they are about breaking the seal of their virginity. It is not too late to hold your virginity in highest esteem, even if you are no longer a virgin.
- **Having your cake:** Anyone can simply live like he or she is married even without signing an actual contract, but in order to receive the supernatural help needed in marriages today, one must embrace covenant.
- **The photo album:** To sacrifice something means to surrender it or to give it up. A picture perfect bride dressed in white can symbolize purity as two friends have waited to sacrifice the seal of their virginity. Unfortunately, 95 percent of us can only take a mental picture, but God can restore.
- **Family ties:** It is important to understand that when two people enter the covenant of marriage, the two extended families become one. The twelve pillars that were erected represented the other parties to the covenant. Moses had to pass these pillars to get to the altar. In the same way, we have to acknowledge the fact that we are not just entering into covenant with our spouses, we are also entering into covenant with both sides of the family.

"In matters of style, swim with the current; in matters of principle, stand like a rock."

Thomas Jefferson

Action Task #2
Guiding Principles

- **Set aside some time to make a list of guiding principles** that you will live by.
- **Make sure you are passionate about these principles** because that passion will help you stand like a rock. A good way to gauge passion is if it hurts when one of your principles are violated.
- **Commit these principles to memory** so that you will always know when to stand like a rock and when to swim with the current. I have a total of five (5) guiding principles and as the domestic head of my home I constantly teach these principles to my wife and kids. In essence, it has become a covenant within my family not to violate our guiding principles.

The In-House Trial

How much can you really learn in 30 days?

Chapter 13

THE IN-HOUSE TRIAL

Try it before you buy it

I often hear single people joke about the misconception that sex inside of marriage is boring and unfulfilling. That statement could not be farther from the truth. Maybe they got this misconception from listening to comedians who joke about how unfulfilling their ex-wives were. Truthfully, the fulfillment of sex inside of marriage is the one experience a single person who has never been married knows nothing about, regardless of how much sex outside of marriage he or she has had. As a matter of debate, there are more factors associated with sex outside of marriage that limit sexual fulfillment than the factors surrounding sex inside of marriage. For instance, mutual faithfulness outside of marriage can limit sexual fulfillment, while greater levels of commitment inside of marriage can increase sexual fulfillment. I like to call sex inside of marriage sex with a purpose because the factors inside of marriage are working towards the purpose of sexual fulfillment. Such factors as mutual love and respect may exist outside of marriage, but sex inside of marriage has a greater sense of commitment that can change the dynamics of sexual fulfillment.

In an article for Parade magazine (March 1994), Dr. Georgia H. Witkin, assistant professor of psychiatry and reproductive sciences at Mount Sinai School of Medicine in New York City, dispels the myth that a long-term sexual relationship breeds discontent. She states, "Most long-term couples do not suffer from sexual boredom," adding that, "When it comes to sex, familiarity breeds contentment rather than boredom." Here are a few other sexual myths I've heard concerning "trying it before you buy it."

- **Experience makes you a better lover:** I've had people ask me, "What if I get married and can't do it right?" I answer that is just an excuse to sow your royal oats! One does not learn how to have sex with a future spouse by collecting sexual experiences with different partners. Our bodies respond to changing environments in a variety of biological and cultural ways. Understand that our sexuality changes overtime as we develop, adjust, and become acclimated to a new sexual environment. Therefore, having had multiple sex partners is experientially useless in finding your sexual groove with your future spouse because the elements needed to achieve sexual fulfillment are not present. Remember the red corvette analogy. In order to get the sexual engines running, married couples must make sure they are hitting on all cylinders. A cylinder is the space in which the hard piston strokes back and forth while riding on a thin layer of lubricating oil. The cylinders have grooves, and the piston will eventually get into the groove overtime. There are mental, emotional, physical, financial and spiritual grooves, to say the least, which must be firing in a marriage. When we have sex outside of marriage we can care less about these grooves, making sex more of a drag race where someone eventually burns out with the same ole fantasy that will never fulfill them. Sex inside of marriage is reality based, where communication about all the elements teaches both partners how to hit on all cylinders, allowing them to stay in the groove and reach maximum fulfillment.

- **My sexual past will not affect my sex life once I'm married:** I do not know your past, but if you have ever been caught up in the game there are several things that we could probably agree on. For instance, the more sexually intimate you are with a person the harder it becomes to get them out of your mind. I believe this is why abused women run back to men who treat them like trash, and even though he does not love her, he still wants her in his life. What an unfortunate paradox it is to have a soul tie that does not simply go away because someone says it is over. These thoughts, emotions, and expectations become more and more fragmented as they transfer from one relationship to the next, making it difficult to bond without sex. If sex is the only thing you have to build a lasting bond with your spouse, then divorce is inevitable.
- **No one wants to marry a virgin anymore:** Why have I heard this excuse so many times? Maybe this is just a guilty comeback statement since 95 percent of Americans have premarital sex according to the national survey of family growth. In theory,

marrying a virgin would be the most perfect way to achieve sexual fulfillment. If two virgins come together in marriage, there is no safer forum where mutual satisfaction can be practiced and unselfish consideration can promote sexual fulfillment. Instead, we spend a large part of our single lives writing our sexual history only to spend a larger part of our married lives trying to erase it. Sexual regret statistics show that 72 percent of sexually active college-aged students, prior to attending an educational program about sexual health issues, have regretted their decision to engage in sexual activity at least once.[52] Trying to unloose the soul ties, mental anguish, past pains, and experiences takes up a huge chunk of time that could be used to connect with our spouses. It is as if we spend our youth with sexual fantasizing, but we spend our marriage trying to get back to a virgin mentality. Unfortunately, not many married couples are willing to work through these past issues, so they divorce and carry the baggage into other relationships. The paradox is that sexual history

> always comes with baggage, but those who do not want to marry a virgin still want their spouses to be free from baggage or carry the lightest load. I've never observed or even heard of a married couple proudly pointing out past sex partners to one another as they stroll through a public place. I believe people want to marry virgins; they just seem to want their virgins to have experience, even though experience does not mean a thing.

The culture of the game has personified the idea of sexual fantasy. Fantasies are being chased like a drug where their temporary fix is mainly a superficial illusion unrestricted by reality. The more we embrace the culture of the game, the more scripted our sexual experience will become. The physical contact and penetration is real, but the response we get from a casual sex partner is mixed with fake *sensationalism*. A recent study showed that many women pretend or "fake" orgasm. One of the study's purposes was to investigate what men's and women's reports of pretending orgasm reveal about their sexual scripts and the functions of orgasms within these scripts.

Participants were 180 male and 101 female college students; 85 percent of the men and 68 percent of the women had experienced penile-vaginal intercourse (PVI). Participants completed a qualitative questionnaire anonymously. Both men (25%) and women (50%) reported pretending orgasm (28% and 67%, respectively for PVI-experienced participants). Frequently reported reasons were that orgasm was unlikely, they wanted sex to end, they wanted to avoid negative consequences (e.g., hurting their partner's feelings), and to obtain positive consequences (e.g., pleasing their partner).[53]

People seem to be learning the cultural fantasy of sex, but two inexperienced married people can learn fulfillment more successfully when there aren't any illusions to unlearn. While we are out trying it before we buy it with person A, B, C, and D, the experiences we are gaining from those sex partners will not apply to persons E through Z because sexual fulfillment is more than a physical act, and only person Z can communicate what fulfills him or her. This is why sexual fulfillment outside of marriage is a moving target. Our sex drives can change as we age, but more importantly, we are continuously discovering ourselves and learning our partner as we age. If person Z finds out that you are wishing he or she would be or respond more like person A, your sexual engine will probably lockup. In light of this reality, maybe you can admit that trying it before you buy it is more about the superficial good time, rather than becoming a better lover for your future spouse.

The next time you are challenged by the misconception that sexual experience makes you a good lover, simply reconsider this PVI statistic, over half the time your sex partners are not telling you the truth about your sexual experiences; therefore, what have you learned? Yes, you may be experienced, but you are experienced at knowing nothing about your future spouse. And if you do get married, the only thing you will know about your spouse is that person A through Y does not apply. If you are only having sex to gain experience, I do not think you would reveal that to your sex partners anyway. Can you imagine someone saying to you "I only want to have sex with you to gain experience for my future spouse?" For some that would be a welcomed fantasy, but for those of us who want a successful relationship, it would be a slap in the face.

The "try it before you buy it" philosophy goes beyond just having sex. Over half of all first marriages are preceded by living together before actually getting married.[54] The reality is that living together may look like a marriage, but cohabitants are not as committed as married couples in their dedication to the continuation of the relationship, and they are more oriented toward their own personal autonomy.[55] According to research that was published by Rutgers University, "Should We Live Together? What Young Adults Should Know about Cohabitation before marriage" the following findings were presented:

> *According to surveys, most young people say it is a good idea to live with a person before marrying. But a careful review of the available social science evidence suggests that living together is not a good way to prepare for marriage or to avoid divorce. Specifically, the research indicates that: Unmarried couples have lower levels of happiness and well being than married couples and living together before marriage increases the risk of breaking up after marriage.*

The same people who say they will never marry someone before trying them out sexually, are the same people included in the epidemic divorce rate. The statistics show that trying it before you buy it will not save you from divorce and does not make a marriage work. When a couple who is used to being with persons A through Z finally settles within the boundaries of marriage, reality settles in as well. And the reality is that you have committed to spending the rest of your life with a person who will never be able to collectively perform as persons A through Z did, because your sex drive has been trained to always want someone different. Moreover, once you get married, the rush will no longer be there because the sex will no longer be forbidden. This reality is partly why spouses cheat. They cheat because they are mentally, physically, and emotionally addicted to chasing after a temporary rush based on fantasy and lust. No matter how hard a spouse tries, he or she will never achieve continuous sexual fulfillment with one life-long partner until those soul ties are broken.

The only thing "trying it before you buy it" teaches is how pretentious sex outside of marriage really was once you experience sex inside of marriage. When the spirit, soul, and body are engaging as one, a couple can achieve continuous sexual fulfillment. Seeing the attraction and charm of your spouse creates a physical connection. Hearing warm, desirable, and endearing words adds to your intimacy. Learning the natural scent that uniquely belongs to your spouse beyond the colognes, perfumes, and lotions creates an arousing identity that draws you to your spouse. Feeling your spouse's hands caressing your body is a touch of acceptance that says my body belongs to you and you alone. When you taste the sweetness of your spouse's kiss it is not distorted by the longing for someone else's lips. Yes, true sexual fulfillment does require a physical connection, but so much more.

I remind you again of the 'soul' which includes our mind, will, and emotions. These elements separate human sexuality from just a blow up doll type fantasy, but the culture of the game can corrupt the mind, destroy the will, and freeze emotions until it brings death to the soul. And when a couple gets married, they can spend years trying to resurrect a dead soul.[56] The unfortunate reality is that marriage is the place where many couples discover this disconnect. For example, a woman's mind weighs everything that goes into the sexual experience. When it is time to have sex with her spouse, her sexual fulfillment is connected to her state of mind. Therefore, if what happens in the marriage bed is not preceded by love, tenderness, understanding, support, help, financial security, peace, etc., then the woman's mind will not be at ease, and sexual relations are likely to be both unfulfilling and infrequent.

Think of it like this, outside of marriage love is more closely related to filling one's soul with shimmering moonbeams on the lily pond when the fragrant lilies are in bloom. Inside of marriage, love is more closely related to filling ones dish sink with the warm suds of liquid Palmolive detergent to clean a pile of fine china before twilight. As men, whether or not we have sex tends to influence many of our everyday decisions and activities. But for women, everyday decisions and activities tend to influence whether or not they even want to have sex. Sex outside of marriage usually disregards this reality, causing couples to have unrealistic expectations that eventually lead to divorce.

Stored up sexual tension can trigger certain emotions such as disappointment or anger, especially in men. If sexual tension exists, but there are other priorities that must be addressed first, some people will become quiet, secluded, and will even lash out. Physical intimacy connects the senses; intimacy of the soul connects us mentally and emotionally, but spiritual intimacy connects us with God. A man and a woman entering such a covenant will not allow sex or their emotions to be the primary factor for marriage.[57] Just as many consented to covenant in biblical days, but did not live up to it, marriages today are failing because we do not understand that covenant is spiritual. I believe Friedrich Nietzsche was getting close to this revelation when he said, “The degree and nature of a man’s sexuality extends to the uppermost pinnacle of his spirit.” No matter how acceptable anal and oral sex becomes in society, no matter how many people opt to simply live together, no matter how many divorces have taken place, and no matter how much sexual perversion the culture of the game promotes, in God’s eyes marriage will always be current, always be superior, always be honorable, and its bed will always be undefiled.

I understand that living together as an alternative to marriage is not likely to go away. Given this reality, one purpose of this chapter has been to shed some light on the "try it before you buy it" misconception. Even if we try a consumer product such as an auto dealer's demo vehicle, or a mattress store's in-house display, when it comes time to buy we want the closest thing to new we can possibly get. Used and refurbished products are cheaper and riskier than a quality new product. When it came to a mate, I personally wanted someone who had not been around the block. How often do we think about the estimated one million people in the U.S. who are living with HIV? Do you ever wonder if you are one out of five Americans who is currently infected with a sexually transmitted disease, but are unaware of their infection as reported by the CDC? Or, are you the average person who only sees the pretty packaging and compelling advertisement that screams, "Take me I'm yours?" Believe it or not, every sexual act we experience outside of marriage will have an impact on our sexual activity inside of marriage.

SHOPPING GUIDE
Sex inside of MARRIAGE

- **Newlyweds:** Even if you have been dating the same person for 20 years, marriage opens up a whole new freedom. Allow the freedom that happens in marriage to open you up for new, continuous, life-long learning, as you both will grow and change together.
- **The Chase:** Some spouses cheat because they are mentally, physically, and emotionally addicted to chasing after a temporary rush based on fantasy and lust. You will never achieve continuous sexual fulfillment with one life-long partner until that addiction is broken.
- **The Honeymoon:** Understand that sexuality changes overtime as we develop, adjust, and become acclimated to our non-honeymoon environments. The marriage bed can be in competition with domestic chores; kids; work schedules; physical, emotional, financial, and spiritual issues. Enhance pleasure by working together to ease the pressure inside and outside the bedroom door.
- **Unpacking Your Lives:** Those who do not want to marry virgins, still want their spouses to be free from baggage, or carry the lightest load. Be willing to work through past experiences and unresolved issues for the good of the marriage.

Going out of business

Isn't quality more important than quantity?

Chapter 14

GOING OUT OF BUSINESS

The Final Sale

Have you ever been in the produce department of a grocery store that had spoiled fruit? Were there fruit flies all around the area? Did it smell fresh and preserved? If you have had a bad fruit experience you probably did not go back to that store again, at least not to buy fruit. This type of experience can cause a grocery store to go out of business while also hurting the consumer. When a grocery store accumulates large volumes of unsold merchandise the perceived quality of those products diminishes, possibly due to the fact that it has been handled and returned so much. Satisfaction and guarantees on such products become void because they have been outside the controls and boundaries that ensured their top quality. In the same way, having no sexual controls and boundaries poses similar risks because insects, discoloration, bruises, and disease can show up in your sexual fruit, and, there may not be an available fix. Aids and certain other STDs can not be returned for a refund, and unfortunately, not everyone will recover from such a loss. It is like having a worthless gift card that can no longer be redeemed. Often it is at the going out of business sale where we finally wake up to the reality that quality was indeed more important than quantity.

At the lowest point in our marriage my wife and I were about to close up shop because we had no foundation and many promises were not being kept. It seemed like our contract was about to expire but frequent counseling sessions granted us a much needed extension. Nothing was working until we stretched out our hand of friendship and began pouring a footing together. We started to build our relationship upon the principles of covenant outlined in chapter 12. As a matter of truth, because I was out of position as the man of the house, the blessing of such a covenant did not flow to me and therefore did not flow to my wife. I have always been a good person seeking to do good works, but I lacked the faith and grace needed to fuel those good works. This revelation led me to spend a season alone with God literally begging for help. After months of alone time communing with God, this is the advice I received: "Give yourself to your wife." This felt like a low blow. I was thinking I spend months with God about my marriage and that is all He has to say! I said, "Ok God, I'm still hurting, but I'll do it." I did not realize it at first, but this was the beginning of spiritual covenant being restored in my marriage.

It took a lot more effort to give myself to my wife than I thought. When I wanted to promote my way over hers, I would here, "Give yourself to your wife." When I wanted to shut down and stone wall, I would hear, "Give yourself to your wife." When I wanted to become angry and lash out, I would hear, "Give yourself to your wife." It felt like my manhood had been taken away from me. At first I felt like a wimp- like I was less than a man. Even then I would hear, "Give yourself to your wife." Then I realized that my marriage was starting to get better. Everything that I gave to my wife she began to give back to me in a much greater way. Every kind word I spoke to her she returned with a kinder word. Every sacrifice I made for her she returned with a greater sacrifice. There was nothing I could do that she did not do greater. I was starting to get why God only said that one sentence. It was a spiritual principle that I had to learn through obedience. "Give yourself to your wife" had nothing to do with being a wimp, but everything to do with being a real man.

When I spent alone time with God, it was a reflection of his order for mankind. Adam spent alone time with God long before his wife Eve came on the seen. My manhood was formed by spending time with God so that He could teach me how to love, how to be kind, how to honor, how to be humble, how not to keep record of wrong, how not to be self-seeking or angry, how to protect, trust, and hope and how to persevere. These are all things God wants the husband to give to the wife. And if men learn to give of themselves from the greatest giver of all times, our wives will give back to us much more, without any trace of being controlled or made to do anything. Just as Adam and Eve were not being controlled by God, neither were my wife and I. We are all compelled to serve because God gave of himself to receive back a world of people. Therefore, since men are the spiritual heads of the home, we must follow God's divine order and give of ourselves to our wives.

This sheds a new light on what it means to be the head. Through the head everything else gets fed, and in return, everything else takes care of the head much more than the head can take care of itself. In the head is vision and leadership that flows down to every other member who helps bring it to pass. The head can lead its members to victory or defeat depending on where he is getting his direction. I can say first hand that giving yourself to your wife is not the easiest direction to follow, but it will be the most rewarding for your marriage. Since I had this encounter with God, I continue to find answers as I seek His guidance for my marriage. I was contractually married in 1998, but for years I did not understand covenant. Today, because of that understanding, we have a very strong confidence that we will keep our commitment, "till death do us part." The ultimate oxymoron is to think that one can have such a spiritual blessing of covenant without including the God who created marriage in the beginning.

Game Over

The success of the AFIEM approach is based on the hope that you will denounce, discern and dodge the game altogether. Many have become so addicted to relationship shopping that they do not know how to declare "Game over." I do not know what it is like to be addicted to nicotine, alcohol, or other drugs, so I asked several smokers and addicts to describe their addiction. One person provided an answer that really stayed with me. He said that when using for the very first time, the initial rush caused a high that he continues to long for, and every time he uses, it is an unsuccessful attempt to reach that first high again. This attempt has been going on for so long that, as the effects of the temporary high wears off, he has to use just to feel normal. Wow! No wonder a person can detoxify from a chemical dependency in weeks, but it can take years to break the mental stronghold. Other research shows that nicotine activates reward pathways which are the part of the brain that regulates feelings of pleasure and *euphoria*. Some smokers say that they feel more relaxed, alert, and less stressed with a cigarette, although the stress levels of adult non-smokers are reportedly lower.

I can not reiterate enough how sexual promiscuity can cause similar strongholds that are deeply rooted in fantasy. So many people have been used, worn, torn, and abused by the game for so long that they even discount themselves well below their original value in one final attempt to lure someone close enough who is willing to look past the damage. More often than not, sex is the bait on their hook and just as a fish can not see the hook, we as people can not see the many hooks that have lodged deep within, pulling us towards sexual experiences that will never fulfill our fantasy. Since fantasies are not real, we find ourselves being lured towards such experiences that will never measure up because we have become programmed to look for new experiences that will take us higher and higher until nothing can fulfill us at all.

Casual sex has the propensity to train your sex drive to be perverted, obsessive, masochistic, sadistic, and addicted. As a result, it can make it harder to train and grow an enjoyable and rewarding sex life in marriage. Sex inside of marriage should be a pleasurable journey that never reaches a plateau. This type of sexual fulfillment does not exist with just a physical experience typically found in sex outside of marriage. This is why pornographic and erotic sex is addictive, but not fulfilling. It trains your sex drive to long for something that does not really exist. Chasing one fantasy after the next is a temporary advance that is purely based on a physical approach to sex. The problem is that every attempt to fulfill such a fantasy causes one to drift further from reality. Sex inside of marriage will never have a fighting chance if your fulfillment expectations are based purely on the physical because we have so many physical limitations. Sex inside of marriage provides the platform not only through physical, mental, emotional, and financial connections; it also provides a spiritual connection that makes it possible to achieve life-long sexual fulfillment. If you go into marriage with a fantasy addiction, reality is going to slap you on both sides of your face before you ever have the chance to know what hit you.

I hope this book has helped take the blinders off so you can see the game for what it really is. I hope you can at least see that the AFIEM approach is a much better way to authenticate a relationship and move toward success. Some of us have been fortunate enough to find someone who is willing to see the treasure and value in us; others are still walking the cluttered shopping isles of hopelessness. Bad experiences may have you feeling worthless like a used Kleenex, but the five words that motivated me to write this book and the five words that motivates me to host seminars are the same five words I want to leave with you in hope that you will be encouraged and motivated to embrace this AFIEM approach. It is simply profound to know that

"YOU ARE WORTH THE EFFORT!" Yes, those are the five words that I want to resonate in you. No matter what you have been through, you are still worth it!

As you continue to view the world as one big shopping mall and every place that you go as a department store of potential mates, you will clearly see that the so called pimps, players, macks, *big ballers*, and shot callers have at some point been returned for a full refund to franchises around the world; they will never be sold out or on back order because they come a dime a dozen. I started this book by explaining that the game is on whether you want it to be or not. I want to end this book having empowered you to say the words "GAME OVER" and mean it. If you truly denounce, discern, dodge the game and take the AFIEM approach seriously, you can literally put the game out of business in your life. I know one bad relationship after another can be devastating, but if I did not think you were worth it, I would not have written this book.

It is not enough that I believe in you, you must also believe in yourself by making those five words personal. Hear is your final action task; say out loud right now, "I AM WORTH THE EFFORT!" Every single day you wake, continue to speak those words. When your established boundaries are being challenged say, "I AM WORTH THE EFFORT!" Think of those words when observed behavior contradicts what was said; speak these words when the wall of communication seems to be getting thicker and taller. It is not about the statistics anymore; it is about how special your life is and how two people who value the truth can put in the effort to bring out the best in one another. Game Over!

Join the initiative to encourage men to value women and inspire women to see themselves as treasures. We hope this book helps you flourish in your relationships.

Five clicks to show your support for this initiative:

1. Join the I Am Worth the Effort companion **blog** entitled, "Monday Morning Motivation." A relevant blog that support the ideas of this book, provide links to helpful resource sites, and interaction through twitter and facebook all in one spot. Click "follow blog via email" to join. www.iamwte.wordpress.com
2. While on our blog site connect with us on **Facebook and Twitter** to receive updates and inspiration in real time.
3. Link from our blog to our **website!** Check out who we are and what we support. **Join our "I Am Worth the Effort Email list"** for periodic updates.
4. While on our website do **sign the guest book**. You are encouraged to share your story to motivate others, read encouraging stories, or simply leave comments about the book. www.iamworththeeffort.com.
5. Finally, if you are motivated by the book, start a Sex Lies & Alibis **Small Group**. You can download a free discussion guide from our website to get started. I will personally be available to your group to address any questions, comments or concerns. Email dwain@iamworththeeffort.com and we will put in the effort together.

Glossary

Amorous: showing, feeling, or inclined to sexual love.

Big Baller: originating from a term referring to a very talented basketball player, typically a pro or from "street ball", who lives lavishly—this phrase is commonly used to refer now to anyone who likes to "live large" (urbandictionary.com)

Culture: the total ways of living built up by a group of human beings and transmitted from one generation to another. The behaviors and beliefs characteristic of a particular social, ethnic, or age group:

Euphoria: an excited state of joy, a good feeling, a state of intense happiness.

Mack: (verb) to hit on, flirt with, or seduce a female by using verbal or sometimes physical means of persuasion. (urbandictionary.com)

Pimp: figuratively used to refer to a person who glorifies being found with lots of women and keeps such women in check through mental and/or physical oppression. (Literal: a man who lives off the earnings of a prostitute or a brothel; a pander.)

Player: (Playa) a person who can deceptively lead on multiple people of the opposite sex into thinking there is a long term relationship in process, when in reality they are just using them for sex, material favors or some other personal fulfillment objective. (urbandictionary.com)

Regenerative: to cause to undergo moral, spiritual, or physical renewal or invigoration. To revive or produce anew; bring into existence again.

Sensationalism: subject matter, language, or style producing or designed to produce startling or thrilling impressions or to excite and please vulgar taste.

Sexism: Attitudes or behavior based on traditional stereotypes of sexual roles. Discrimination or devaluation based on a person's sex, as in discrimination directed against women.

Shot caller: Someone who calls the shots. 2. Someone who demands control due to an elevated social status. (urbandictionary.com)

Sovereignty: having supreme rank, power, or authority that is excellent and effective.

Virtuous: conforming to moral and ethical principles; morally excellent; upright.

Womanizing : to pursue or chase women habitually. To indulge in many casual affairs with women.

Endnotes

[1] Latest Hong Kong, China & World News I SCMP.com. (n.d.). Retrieved from www.scmp.com/portal/site/SCMP/menuitem.06f0b401397a029733492d9253a0a0a0?v...

[2] Galatians 5:14-24

[3] 1 Thessalonians 5:23

[4] Bargh, J. A., & Chartrand, T. L. (in press). Studying The Mind in the Middle: A practical guide to priming and automaticity research. In H. Reis & C. Judd (eds.), *Research methods in social psychology.* New York: Cambridge University Press.

[5] 1 Timothy 4:2

[6] Romans 8:16

[7] "Porn Profits: Corporate America's Secret." Abcnews.go.com. N.p., n.d. Web. 23 Aug. 2011

[8] John 8:32. "And ye shall know the truth, and the truth shall make you free." John 8:44 (New Living Translation) "For you are the children of your father the devil, and you love to do the evil things he does. He was a murderer from the beginning and has always hated the truth. There is no truth in him." Romans 3:4 (New Living Translation) "… Though everyone else <u>in the world</u> is a liar, God is true…" Psalms 119:160 "the word is true from the beginning..." John 17:17 "Sanctify them through the truth: the word is truth." John 16:13 "the Spirit of truth will guide you into <u>all truth</u>…"

[9] Matthew 11:18 (New Living Translation)

[10] About 11 percent of murder victims between 1976 and 2002 were killed by their spouses or lovers, according to the U.S. Department of Justice.

[11] Revelation 12:9 the devil and Satan is the old serpent.

[12] Colossians 2:3 "…in whom are hidden all the treasures of wisdom and knowledge;" 1 Corinthians 1:30 "But of Him you are in Christ Jesus, who became for us wisdom from God--and righteousness and sanctification and redemption-- "

[13] "How the Bible Made America," *Newsweek*, December 1982

[14] John 3:16

[15] Luke 4:18 "The Spirit of the Lord is upon me, because he hath anointed me to preach the gospel to the poor; he hath sent me to heal the brokenhearted, to preach deliverance to the captives, and recovering of sight to the blind, to set at liberty them that are bruised."

[16] Proverbs 3:13; Proverbs 28:14; Job 5:7; Psalms 127:5

[17] Romans 7:23

[18] 1 Corinthians 15:26 and Hebrews 2:14 Satan had the power of death

[19] John 12:32

[20] Psalms 133:2

[21] The New Strong's Exhaustive concordance of The Bible. James Strong, LL.D., S.T.D.

[22] Source: Quote captured from BET's documentary featuring rap artist Trina.

[23] Galatians 5:22-23

[24] Proverbs 29:18

[25] Proverbs 10:22

[26] Romans 1:31

[27] John 14:15 KJV

[28] John 13:35 (New Living translation)

[29] Colossians 4:5-6

[30] Santagati, Steve. 2007. The MANual. New York, NY: Crown Publishing.
[31] Daily, Lisa. "Dating Averages: What's Your Normal?" Canoe.ca. September 18, 2009.
[32] Langer, Gary. "Poll: American Sex Survey." ABCNews.com. October 21, 2004.
[33] Judges chapters 13, 14, 15 and 16.
[34] Weitzman's The Divorce Revolution (1985)
[35] Matthew 11:29 (KJV)
[36] John 15:13(KJV)
[37] 1 John 4:17(New King James Version)
[38] Hebrews 13:5
[39] Matthew 1:18-25
[40] The New Strong's Exhaustive Concordance of The Bible. The KJV New Testament Greek Number 4905, sunerchomai.
[41] Deuteronomy 20:7; Luke 1:56; Deuteronomy 22:23, 24 & Genesis 38:24.
[42] NIV Matthew 1:20-25
[43] 1 Samuel chapters 18, 20 and 2 Samuel 21:7
[44] Ezekiel 16:8 and Hosea 2:16
[45] Exodus 24:3-8
[46] Exodus 20:24
[47] The New Strong's Exhaustive Concordance of The Bible. The KJV Old Testament Hebrew Numbers 5769 and 410. Gen 21:33; Isa 9:6; Isa 40:28
[48] Genesis 9:16; Genesis 17:7
[49] Exodus 24:11 Mount Sinai
[50] Psalms 50:5
[51] Exodus 24:8
[52] Oswalt SB, Cameron KA, Koob JJ. Sexual Regret in College Students. Arch Sex Behavior. 2005 Dec;34(6):663-9. PubMed PMID: 16362250.

[53] The Department of Psychology and Women, Gender, and Sexuality studies at the University of Kansas. Muehlenhard CL, Shippee SK. Men's and Women's Reports of Pretending Orgasm. J Sex Res. 2010 Nov; 47(6):552-67. PubMed PMID: 19707929.
[54] Larry Bumpass and Hsien-Hen Lu. 1998. "Trends in Cohabitation and Implications for Children's Family Contexts." Unpublished manuscript, Madison, WI: Center for Demography, University of Wisconsin. The most likely to cohabit are people aged 20 to 24.
[55] Stephen L. Nock. 1995. “A Comparison of Marriages and Cohabiting Relationships.” Journal of Family issues 16-1:53-76. See also: Robert Schoen and Robin M Weinick. 1993. “Partner Choice in Marriages and Cohabitations.” Journal of Marriage and the Family 55:408-414.
[56] Ezekiel 18:4
[57] 1corinthians 7:37
[58] Christianity Today, October 26, 1992, p. 30 The Barna survey asked, “Is there absolute truth?” 66 percent of American adults said no. The figure rises to 72 percent when it comes to those between the ages of 18 and 25.

About The Author

L. Dwain Boswell is the founder of iamworththeeffort.com, an initiative to encourage both men and women to take a new approach to successful relationships. He is a faithful husband and devoted father who believes valuing women is a responsibility that comes with being a real man. As an author and speaker, he uses his talent to bring awareness to the dark and evil abomination of human trafficking and the mindless exploitation of women. He believes that half the battle of solving any problem is exposing it, and for over 15 years has been passionate about inspiring a generation of men who will join the movement of treasuring our women and girls. Dwain has been married to Renona for nearly 14 of those years. They have two children and live in the beautiful state of Alabama. You can contact Dwain through the web site mentioned above.

www.ingramcontent.com/pod-product-compliance
Lightning Source LLC
Chambersburg PA
CBHW060838280326
41934CB00007B/828

* 9 7 8 0 9 8 4 8 6 6 7 4 8 *